W9-BVP-632

Brain Gain

How innovative cities create job growth in an age of disruption

By Robert Bell, John Jung & Louis Zacharilla

Published by the
Intelligent Community Forum
www.intelligentcommunity.org

First edition, published by Intelligent Community Forum
250 Park Avenue, 7th Floor, New York, NY 10177 USA
+1 646-291-6166, fax +1 212-825-0075 www.intelligentcommunity.org

Table of Contents

Brain Gain

Shoutout

This publication is made possible by the contributions of many people and institutions around the world. Without their support, both financial and intellectual, the Intelligent Community movement could not spread its ideas and tell these stories of risk, perseverance and success, nor continue our global dialogue to influence the future of cities, towns, regions and the nations where they lie.

A special acknowledgement goes to the following organizations, whose financial support enabled the publication of *Brain Gain*:

- **Chunghwa Telecom**
- **The Columbus Region**
- **Greater Columbus Arts Council**
- **Industrial Development & Investment Promotion Committee of Taichung, Taiwan**
- **Oulu, Finland, Capital of Northern Scandinavia**
- **RBC Royal Bank**
- **City of Stratford, Ontario, Canada**
- **Taoyuan Metropolis, Taiwan**
- **University of Waterloo / Stratford**
- **Vee Time Corp.**
- **Waterfront Toronto**

Special acknowledgement also goes to Professors Don Flournoy and Faith Knutsen of Ohio University, Sylvie Albert of the University of Winnipeg, Michael Dunphy of Walsh University, Tomoko Kanayama of Komazawa University,

Cheol-Soo Park of Sungkunkwan University, Matthias Takouda of Laurentian University, and Mr. Jagadish Rao, all of whom have been instrumental to our understanding and evaluation of Intelligent Communities.

Thanks also to Dr. Norman Jacknis, our Senior Fellow, who is helping to bring the ICF message and method to the rural sectors in an effort to turn brain drain into brain gain.

We wish to also congratulate Jackie DeGarmo, the executive director of the world's first-ever Institute for the Study of the Intelligent Community at Walsh University in North Canton, Ohio, USA. It is a place where the world can study the educational methods and programs of the world's most successful communities.

ICF thanks its international jury, made up of citizens from all walks of life around the globe. These men and woman on every continent spend precious time each year to ensure that the Top7 receive a fair hearing as they pursue the Intelligent Community of the Year honor.

Finally, we acknowledge the civic leaders and citizens of the world's 126-and-counting Intelligent Communities. Without their dedication, courage and bold pursuit of ideas for rebuilding communities, we would have no stories to tell and the places we call home would not have so bright future as we believe they will.

Authors' Preface

Nearly twenty years ago, in 1995, four hundred people from different countries assembled in Toronto to celebrate something called "Smart." The event was not about IQ, nor was it a fashion show. Smart '95 was about how the booming field of telecommunications – and in particular, this relatively new thing called the internet – might impact the development of economies at the local level.

One of our authors, John Jung, organized Smart '95 to provide a meeting place for a nonprofit on whose Board he served. Our other authors, Robert and Lou, helped manage that nonprofit. The conference, held at the dawn of the internet age, attracted telecom people, real estate executives, political leaders, technology gurus, Big Thinkers and even a rock band. Its success signaled that something interesting was happening at the intersection of the digital and physical in the place we call home.

It was also the starting point for the Intelligent Community Forum. We did not know it at the time, but that event lit a spark in us that grew slowly into flame.

For John, an urban planner by training, it was about sharing his vision of new technological and economic influences that would fundamentally transform the city. For Robert, it was a quest to truly understand how the internet would change – for good and for ill – the ways we live, do business and govern ourselves and our societies. For Lou, it was a search for the answer to a question: why his little hometown in northern New York State had, in just one generation, gone from a stable and close-knit community to one in profound economic and social distress.

When a new kind of internet access called broadband was first introduced at the turn of the century, we were invited to do a comparison study of broadband in communities in the US, Canada and UK. The result was a framework for understanding how cities and regions can best use broadband and information technology for economic and social development. We called them the Intelligent Community Factors. They soon became the basis for the international Intelligent Community Awards – and a whole lot more.

Since then, Mayors, City Councilors, economic development officers, "new urbanism" planners, nonprofits and foundations have adopted them as the foundation for growing local economies in this century of disruption. We have been invited to places we could only have imagined – from Finland, Australia and China to the 2012 Nobel Peace Prize – to talk about Intelligent Communities and their contribution to prosperity, inclusion and more open societies.

Technology has been the starting place for those discussions, but they now range far beyond to all the critical factors in the life of a community. We have received the support of many technology companies along the way, and we commend their efforts to create smarter cities. "Smart" is just as good an idea today as it was in 1995. In Smart Cities, things work better. But in Intelligent Communities, people live better, and that is what *Brain Gain* is all about.

Many of the people involved in our work are based in one of the more than 125 Intelligent Communities recognized by ICF's award program around the world. You will meet many of them in the pages of *Brain Gain.* In particular, you will meet the Top7 Intelligent Communities of 2013 and read many stories about their challenges and the remarkable ways in which those challenges were addressed. The communities are Columbus, Ohio in the USA; Stratford and Toronto in Ontario, Canada; Oulu, Finland and Tallinn, Estonia in Europe; and Taichung City and Taoyuan Metropolis in Taiwan.

You will also read other stories of award-winning cities and regions in Australia, the Netherlands, Portugal, the United Kingdom, the US and Canada. Our emphasis on stories is no accident. When it comes to making people's lives better, facts and figures can only get you so far. Stories of struggle, of fear in the face of uncertainty, of faith and perseverance are far more powerful than statistics or strategies in inspiring action. For inspiring action is also what *Brain Gain* sets out to do.

The communities you read about here have taken risks, just as we did in Toronto in 1995. These Mayors, Councilors, administrative leaders and community champions are the new social entrepreneurs of the age, and the social capital they generate will still be producing a return on investment twenty years from now. Intelligent Communities are the story of our time, and we again have the privilege of telling their stories as we begin together the third decade of this amazing journey.

> Robert Bell, John Jung & Louis Zacharilla
> Co-Founders, Intelligent Community Forum

CHAPTER ONE

Work and Well-Being

In English, short words tend to pack the biggest punch. The little words, with deep roots among the Angles and Saxons living in Britain a millennium ago, are the ones that count. Words like love and hate, life and death.

"Work" is one of them. To work is to direct your physical or mental energy toward a goal and, in its most common usage, to get paid for doing so. Work, in other words, is a job. Work is also the product of that job: your body of work, which reflects what you put into it. Because of this reflecting tendency, work has a way of standing for who you are. "What do you do for a living?" is one of the more common cocktail party conversation starters, when it can be asked without appearing too nosy, because what people do for a living – the activity to which they devote most of their waking hours – usually tells us a great deal about them.

For the person who buys your labor, work is something else. It is the value you can add to a product, service or process. The value may be cleaning and preparing a compli-cated machine, answering phones or loading boxes; it may be teaching, conducting research or managing an organization. Whatever the value you provide, businesses have an unshakeable rule enforced by the pressures of the market. The value you provide must at least justify the cost of your wage, compared with other ways the business could spend money to accomplish the same thing. As we will see in the next chapter, that raises issues of critical importance to towns, cities and regions seeing to build a better life for their citizens.

For the worker, however, work involves another kind of value. Work is how you make a living – but where the human spirit is concerned, it is much more. In the words of the man who gave us the term "knowledge work," the late management consultant Peter Drucker, "To make a living is no longer enough. Work also has to make a life." [1]

Whether we like it or not, for most people, the value we provide through our work, the value reflected in the wage we are paid, is also a measure of our value as a human being.

A 2011 worldwide survey by Gallup showed that people who are employed full-time for an employer tend to have the highest well-being in the workforce. Based on an accepted scale of personal well-being, which rates people as "thriving," "struggling" or "suffering," 29% of full-time employees worldwide were rated as "thriving," compared with 22% employed part-time and seeking additional work or unemployed. Looking just at the advanced economies of the world, Gallup found 52% of full-time employees to be "thriving," compared with 49% of part-timers looking for additional work and 31% of the unemployed. The study concludes that employment status is "one of the most important contributors to a person's well-being." [2]

All jobs, of course, are not created equal. There are bad companies to work for and bad bosses to report to. A lot of them, as it turns out. Teresa Amible, a professor at Harvard Business School, and Steven Kramer, an independent researcher, wrote a book called *The Progress Principle* based on 12,000 electronic diary entries from 238 knowledge workers in seven companies. One-third of the entries expressed frustration, unhappiness, lack of motivation or outright disgust. In analyzing the specific workday events reported in the diaries, a pattern emerged. Guess what people wanted most from their jobs? An office with more windows? A bigger salary? Free pizza and movie nights with the whole team?

What people wanted most of all was simply to make progress in work in which they saw meaning. When workers experienced their labor as meaningful and saw progress toward a goal, they felt more positive and more engaged, and these positive emotions tended to drive deeper engagement.

The authors then asked hundreds of managers at companies around the world to rank in order the things they thought motivated their employees. "Supporting progress" ranked dead last: only 5 percent recognized that making progress in meaningful work is the most powerful motivator in their toolkit. The cheapest motivator, too. How much does it cost to explain why a particular project is important, to give employees the authority to get it done, help them navigate around obstacles and praise them when they do a good job?

Of the seven companies studied, only one had managers who did it right most of the time. It was the only company to achieve a technological breakthrough during the months devoted to the study.

We All Need a Place to Go

Working at a bad job is bad. Having no job, however, is worse. In September 2009, at the height of the financial crisis in the US, the John J. Heldrich Center for Workforce Development at Rutgers University released *The Anguish of Unemployment*, a study based on surveys of 1,200 people currently or recently unemployed. Overwhelming majorities of the survey's respondents reported feeling anxiety, helplessness and depression. They experienced sleeping problems and strained relationships and found themselves steering clear of social situations where their lack of a job might be revealed. One of the study's authors predicted that the impact of the downturn would be felt long after the economy rebounded. "This is a major life-changing experience for people," he says. "It's not like getting over a cold – it's like recovering from serious illness." [3]

Las Vegas resident Donna McGuinn is a walking advertisement for the critical importance of high-level skills in the economy of the 21st Century. A former casino cage worker, she has a secondary school diploma but is uncomfortable around computers and has little else in terms of marketable skills. After being laid off in the Great Recession and applying for hundreds of jobs, she told a blogger for PsychCentral.com:

Unemployment just leads to more homelessness, more depression and the suicide rates will keep going up. You lose something when you don't feel worthy. I've gone two years without a job, and there's no one in your life to say you're doing good. We all need a place to go, a place that makes you feel productive and good about yourself. We all do.[4]

This is an American story, from a place where the social safety net is weak by industrialized world standards and unemployment imposes severe financial hardship and loss of access to regular medical care. But the value of work, and the corrosive effects of being denied it, are universal.

Much of the European Union has severe problems with youth unemployment. In 2012, according to the Organization for Economic Cooperation and Development (OECD), youth unemployment rates were higher than 20% in most of Europe and above 50% in Spain and Greece. A five-year research project suggests that when young Swedes – who enjoy strong income and health support – are unable to find work, it reduces self-confidence and creates feelings of isolation, sometimes leading to clinical signs of anxiety and depression[5] A study published in the *British Medical Journal* stated that the financial crisis led some 5,000 people in 54 countries to commit suicide, with the largest jump in the suicide rate happening among European men age 15-24.[6]

Lack of work carries costs beyond the individual and psychological. It affects communities as well. Research dating back to the Great Depression found that men who experience substantial financial loss become irritable, tense, and explosive. Their children suffer as fathers become more punitive and arbitrary in parenting, and the result is a jump in temper tantrums, irritability, feelings of inadequacy and negativity. The unemployed are also less likely to marry and more likely to divorce than the fully employed, and report less neighborhood belonging. One six-country study found that higher neighborhood unemployment rates are associated with an increased risk of mortality. [7]

Some of these impacts are lessened by a strong social safety net. A 2010 study by three Spanish academics, Rosa Martínez, Jesús Ruiz-Huerta and Luis Ayala, compared unemployment and poverty rates across the OECD countries . They found that, in countries with very generous income support systems like Belgium and Denmark, fewer than 7% of households whose head was unemployed were below the poverty line. In the US and UK, the figure was above 40%. Unemployment benefits reduced poverty rates among the unemployed by +90% in Belgium and Denmark, compared with 49% in the UK and 13% in the US. [8]

Get Me Out of Here

In places where high unemployment and poverty go hand-in-hand, the impact is severe: underfunded schools, the decline of housing stock, and cutbacks to recreation, transportation and services. Windsor, Ontario, Canada lies across a river and an international boundary from Detroit, Michigan, USA. The connections between the two communities run deeper than the chilly currents of the Detroit River. During the post-war decades when Motor City dominated the world auto industry, Windsor became an extension of Detroit's economy. Dozens of automotive assembly plants sprang up on the Canadian side of the border within a 100-mile radius with Windsor at its center. They fed the growth of tool & die works, plastic molding companies, electrical and electronic manufacturers and makers of all the thousands of other parts that go into an automobile.

In 2005, after decades of decline in American automotive manufacturing, the Big Three began a wave of plant closing and mass layoffs. Over the next two years, Windsor lost 17,000 jobs in auto assembly and parts manufacturing, with C\$2 billion in economic impact. Each of those jobs supported another 3 to 4 in retailing, food, construction and public services, and those losses raised the damage by another billion dollars. [9]

That billion-dollar figure masked a kind of death by a thousand cuts. The Windsor Minor Hockey Association had to sharply reduce the number of teams it fielded, with three-quarters of parents who said they would not be registering their kids for hockey citing job loss as the reason. The association was forced to cut its rental of ice time by 12 hours per week, which cost the city \$50,000 in recreational fees. The annual United Way fundraising campaign for charities, traditionally led by the Big Three and the Canadian Auto

Workers union, saw contributions fall 30% from 2001 to 2008.[10]   Canada's income support system delivers poverty reduction at about the same level as the UK but the impact on community life was still profound.

One of those impacts is out-migration. When economic opportunity declines severely enough, citizens vote with their feet. The Windsor region suffered net out-migration of 10,000 people from 2006 to 2011.[11]   More than 280,000 people age 30 and under left Spain in 2012, and a recent European Commission study found that 68% of their peers still in-country were considering moving abroad.[12]   Those who do decide to seek their fortune elsewhere are typically the ones a city, region or nation can least afford to lose: those with marketable skills searching for a market, the risk-takers, the ones with imagination and the willingness to dare. That brain drain can have consequences that last for decades.

Recessions eventually end and the cyclical downturn in employment gradually reverses until economic growth restores things to what we feel is normal. The availability of jobs grows from famine to feast, periods of unemployment shrink from years to months. Secondary and university students no longer look at graduation day as a sentence to purgatory.

But there are disturbing signs that not all of our employ-ment challenges are part of the business cycle. In this inno-vative century, indicators point to greater and ongoing dis-ruption in employment, with all of the impact on individuals and communities it will bring. Rather than being cyclical, disruption may be woven into the fabric of our lives, and the very forces that drive employment growth for some may increasingly undermine job opportunities for the rest.

CHAPTER TWO

Creator, Preserver, Destroyer

Devout Hindus see the operation of the universe through the primal balance among their faith's three leading deities: Brahma the Creator, Vishnu the Preserver and Shiva the Destroyer. Life brings things into being, life nurtures and preserves them, and life inevitably wipes the world of them.

Today, economists ascribe similar powers to create, preserve and destroy to a human activity that dates to the first time our African ancestors used the thigh bone of an antelope to kill their prey. *Innovation*.

To innovate means literally to renew or change something. Innovation is about coming up with a better process, creating a new product, improving an existing one, opening a new market, finding a new source of supply or a creating a better way to organize ourselves. Innovation may be technology-driven today but it is just as likely to focus on a new and better way for people to work together.

Why is innovation a hot topic right now? Simply enough, we believe it to be the primary driver of economic growth – and after years of recession across the industrialized world, growth is a top priority. Innovation turns out to be surprisingly hard to measure, however, as it flows through ideas and experiments into services and products. We owe our understanding of its value to a remarkable Stanford University economist named Moses Abramovitz. [13]

Search for the X-Factor

Back in the 1950s, he decided to test economic theory on some real-world data. He set out to track the growth in the total output of the American economy from 1870 to 1950, and to analyze what caused it. It was a mighty undertaking in those days of paper records and mechanical calculators, but he got it done.

Economic theory of the time said that there are two kinds of inputs to the economy: capital and labor. Capital is the money invested by businesses, institutions and government. Labor is the people they employ. You invest a few million dollars or Euros or pounds in a factory and raw materials. You hire hundreds of workers to staff it. Out of the factory come products and out of the economy comes growth.

Abramovitz assembled his data and was able to produce figures for the total output of the economy between those years. Then he measured the growth in the classic inputs – the total amount of money being invested and the total workforce – over the same period.

With two herculean tasks behind him, Professor Abramovitz then made what he thought were reasonable assumptions about how the much this growth in capital and labor inputs should add to the output of the economy. Growth in A plus growth in B equals growth in C. Simple, right?

Not so much. It turned out that the growth of inputs between 1870 and 1950 could only account for about 15% of the actual growth in economic output. Eighty-five percent of the growth was coming from some X-Factor and neither Professor Abramovitz nor anybody else could say what it might be.

It was a huge wake-up call to economists. It was like having a structural engineer tell you that she really couldn't explain why the Eiffel Tower was still standing. By 1987, the search for the X-Factor earned Professor Robert Solow the Nobel Prize in Economics for demonstrating that the introduction of new technology was responsible for *as much as of 80% of the growth in a nation's gross domestic product.* No less an authority than the management consultant Peter Drucker wrote that the *only* business activities that actually create value are innovation (making something new) and marketing (finding a way to sell it). Everything else a business does – all of its visible aspects from buildings to assembly lines – just costs them money. [14]

The latest research backs up this notion. A 2008 study of innovation in Germany, France, Spain and the UK concluded that "in manufacturing as well as in the service sector, product innovations have a positive impact on gross employment in innovating firms." The authors found that sales growth of 1% due to new products leads to a 1% increase in gross employment. [15]

Winners and Losers

By now, we all accept the vital importance of innovation in growing our economy – despite the fact that innovation *destroys* jobs as well as creating them. In 1900, the second most common occupation in the United States was being a domestic servant. The introduction of labor-saving devices in the home reduced domestic servitude to a statistical blip by the end of the century.

The rest of the 20th Century was to see an amazing advance of innovation and subsequent obsolescence. The success of the mass-produced automobile gradually destroyed all of the production and services related to horse-drawn transportation. The introduction of electronic calculators wiped out production of the mechanical calculators on which Professor Abramovitz did his work. The computer replaced the typewriter – and so much more. Digital music all but eliminated vinyl records, digital video closed thousands of movie rental stores, and email sidelined both fax machines and snail mail, causing a funding crisis for postal services. Yet despite all the losers created by innovation, the success of the winners and the greater value delivered by The Next Big Thing kept making the economy grow.

A *BusinessWeek* study from 2007 concluded that innovative companies achieve average growth in profits of 3.4% per year, compared with 0.4% for the S&P Global 1200. Do that every year for a few years, and the difference becomes massive.

Growing economies need people to work in them, and the wages they are paid not only support the worker who receives them but also accelerate through the economy, creating jobs for other workers. This is the employment "multiplier effect" well known to economic development professionals. Or in a phrase that may have originated with American President John F. Kennedy, it is an example of how "a rising tide lifts all boats."

But it turns out that the connection between innovation and employment growth is more complicated that it seems. Changes in the global economy over the past two decades have created the real possibility that, in the rising tide of the 21st Century, some boats may rise a lot faster than others.

Innovation and Job Polarization
Throughout the developed nations of the world, policymakers are increasingly concerned about something called "job polarization." The term was coined by economists led by David Autor of the Massachusetts Institute of Technology. Two colleagues, Maarten Goos and Alan Manning, extended

the research to Britain and gave it a sexier name: the rise of "lousy and lovely" jobs:

> *Thanks to technology, more and more 'routine' tasks can be done by machines. The most familiar example is the increasing automation of manufacturing. But machines can now do 'routine' white-collar jobs, too — things like the work that used to be performed by travel agents and much of the legal 'discovery' that was done by relatively well-paid associates with expensive law degrees.*
>
> *The jobs that are left are the 'lovely' ones, at the top of the income distribution — white-collar jobs that cannot be done by machines, like designing computer software or structuring complex financial transactions. A lot of 'lousy' jobs are not affected by the technology revolution, either — nonroutine, manual tasks like collecting the garbage or peeling and chopping onions in a restaurant kitchen.* [16]

In other words, there is a tier of occupations at the top where machines are not able – yet – to replicate the mix of knowledge, experience, judgment and intuition that highly educated human beings can deliver. There is another tier of occupations at the bottom, consisting of manual tasks that it does not pay to automate – yet – or that require considerable interaction with human beings, something machines still do poorly. In between are routine and semi-routine jobs that have a bullseye on their backs when it comes to automation.

But wait – it gets worse, according to work by Nir Jaimovich and Henry Siu, economists at Duke University and the University of British Columbia respectively. They suggest that "job polarization isn't a slow, evolutionary process. Instead, it happens in short, sharp bursts…Those spurts of change are economic downturns: Dr. Jaimovich and Dr. Siu have found that in the United States since the mid-1980s, 92 percent of job loss in routine, middle-skill occupations has happened within 12 months of a recession. Dr. Siu described for *The New York Times* the big puzzle about recent business cycles: "Why have we had these jobless recoveries over the past three recessions? These jobless recoveries are because you have these middle-skilled jobs that are being wiped off the table." [17]

Blame ICT

What makes it possible to automate more of those middle-skill jobs every year? Three little letters: ICT or information and communications technology.

The explosive progress of ICT, delivering ever faster, more powerful applications and making them instantly available over broadband, affects everyone from bank tellers (victims of ATMs) to payroll clerks (victims of software and cloud-based services). Those were just two of the many middle-skilled job categories that were found to be most vulnerable to automation in a study by MIT's David Autor and David Dorn of the Centre for Monetary and Financial Studies in Madrid, based on US Department of Labor data from 1980 to 2005. [18]

When it comes to job polarization, ICT is like the proverbial butterfly flapping its wings in the Amazon jungle and, by a chaotic sequence of unpredictable events, stirring up a hurricane in the South Atlantic.

A previous generation of factory workers was reduced in ranks by manufacturing automation and robotics. Today, ICT shifts the target to many categories of middle-skilled knowledge workers: secretaries, data entry clerks, call center operators, paralegals and bookkeepers. As ICT-based applications become cheaper and more powerful, people working in these jobs can no longer deliver enough value to the enterprise to justify the cost of their salary, benefits, training and physical support. This applies even to people on a path to becoming high-priced knowledge workers but who need more training and experience in order to justify what they are paid. American law schools are now being challenged to reduce the number of graduates that they have been so profitably pouring into a market. Why? Because, in 2012, only 55% could expect to find work in the law, as automation eliminated much of the grunt work where young attorneys cut their teeth. [19]

Which points to another seismic shift spurred by ICT. It gives serious economic advantage to those with the skills to use it to increase the value of their work to the employer. Yet another study, this one from the London School of Economics (LSE), used data from nine European countries, Japan and the US for the years from 1980 to 2004. It found that industries that adopted ICT at faster rates (as measured by their spending on ICT and R&D) also saw the fastest growth in demand for the most educated workers and the sharpest declines in demand for people with intermediate levels of education. [20]

Butterfly wings into hurricanes: it turns out that one of the big drivers of ICT adoption is…ICT adoption. That is, as investment in ICT makes companies more competitive, it spurs other companies to do the same in order not to fall behind. Another LSE study looked at a unique moment in history, when China was granted entry into the World Trade Organization and saw trade barriers for its products entering Europe automatically fall. IT adoption rates in Europe jumped from 2000 to 2007, and the study concluded that 15% of technology upgrading could be explained entirely by the increased competition from the Chinese economic juggernaut. When they feel the hot breath of competitors on the backs of their necks, executives invest in ICT and R&D to increase innovation and reduce costs. [21]

Globalization has one further impact on job markets around the world. Companies and individuals that are capable of selling across global markets can reap rewards such as the world has never seen. In 2000, Toyota's annual revenues were $5.8 billion and the pre-iPod Apple made about $5.3 billion. Only eleven years later, the two companies had annual revenues of $236bn and $108bn, respectively, and were far outrun by resource giants like ExxonMobil ($489bn) and BP ($386bn). [22]

Actor Tom Cruise made $75 million in just one year ending May 2012 from standing, running, jumping, punching and glowering in front of a camera.[23] J.K. Rowling, who had to live in her car before publication of the first Harry Potter novel, is the first author in history to earn a billion dollars from her work. [24]

By contrast, the chief executives of the 500 biggest companies in the US took home a paltry total of $5.2bn in salary and bonuses in 2011.[25] And European CEOs were paid only about 40% of that, on average, though executive compensation has risen sharply in the past 10 years as European firms have had to compete globally for talent.

This phenomenon goes by the name of the Winner-Take-All Economy, and has spawned books and articles by the score. The winners are the fabled 1% of Occupy Wall Street fame, for whom globalization has been an unalloyed blessing.

Why It Matters

Put all of this together, and you have a recipe for major social and political strains, as the divide widens between people at the top and bottom of the economic pyramid, and technology change erodes the livelihoods of those in the middle.

Concerns about job polarization have gone viral – a Google search will yield about 3 million hits. Hardly the 37 million that a search for the Eurovision song contest produces, but still impressive for a wonky topic.

It matters so much because middle-skilled jobs are the foundation on which local, regional and national economies rest. In the European Union, medium-skilled jobs made up about 50% of the total in 2010, comparable to the 48% of total American jobs they comprised in 2006.

These middle-skilled jobs generally require some education and training beyond high school but less than a bachelor's degree. It may be an associate's degree from a community college or certificate from a technical school. It may be on-the-job training, previous work experience or just some years at university that did not result in a diploma. Middle-skilled workers are construction supervisors, electricians and plumbers, office administrators, technical salespeople, medical technicians and dental hygienists, telecom equipment installers, welders and first responders.

If middle-skilled jobs are indeed being "wiped off the table" by innovation in information and communications technology, it poses a terrible threat to the economic and social well-being of communities around the world. If rising incomes are highly concentrated in 1-2% of the population while the rest of us get poorer, the developed nations of the world will come to bear a startling resemblance to those chaotic countries at the bottom of the income ladder, where despots or oligarchies control most assets and everyone else lives off their table scraps. Karl Marx, call your office.

When Menial Labor Isn't Menial

If you make a forecast and want to make certain it is dead wrong, there is one guaranteed method: take a trend from today and draw it out for five or ten years in a straight line. Societies, cultures and communities adapt. The high rate of technology change today may be challenging that adaptability, but the story is far from over.

Job polarization is clearly happening – but is it a crisis? In the US, the rate of decline in middle-skilled jobs has been about 0.6% per year since the start of the ICT revolution in the mid-1980s. [26] As professors Jaimovich and Siu have shown, it surges in recessions, then declines in times of growth, but the overall trend has been steady.

Put another way, the slow decline in middle-skilled knowledge-based jobs – those that do not require a physical presence in a particular location – is inevitable. It was inevitable in manufacturing as soon as the first automated machinery was put into place, which is why those Luddites in 19th Century England who destroyed automated looms knew just what they were doing, though they did not do themselves any good. As the Industrial Revolution continues in digital form, we are increasingly capable of automating jobs that require not just a strong back but a bit of knowledge and judgment as well. So, we are doing it. We may well want government to have a policy response, but the best that laws and regulations can do is to cushion change while job markets adapt.

There is another change, however, that has gone little noticed until recently but which is every bit as profound:

> *We have come to expect more from our businesses without noticing the ramifications it has on the skill sets needed to perform these jobs. We want goods and services faster, at cost-effective prices, and with improved customer service. Today's delivery person confirms orders and shipments of goods using a tablet; the shelf stocker no longer places stickers on products,*

but rather uses a complex personal digital assistant device to control stock supplies; and your local coffee shop barista not only serves your coffee, but is also expected to troubleshoot the Wi-Fi. These new responsibilities are no longer the exceptions, but rather the rules...The direct result of companies keeping pace with technological advancements has meant that positions previously requiring low skills now demand solid digital skills: the ability to access, use and interpret digital information in the workplace. [27]

In this view, the really big change is not our increasing ability to automate away routine middle-skill jobs. The really big change is in those non-routine, manual, menial occupations that are traditionally considered low-skilled. The authors of a report called *Menial is Menial No More* put it this way: in the past, for entry level jobs in the hospitality industry, "workers only needed to show up at a hotel seeking work, and as long as they were responsible and reliable, they were fit for the job...Today workers must independently complete an online application process before they are even considered for an interview. At one hotel chain all staff must pass an online customer service course, while another chain requires all cleaning staff to operate a PDA." [28]

Today's job polarization studies forecast that high-skilled positions will see most of the growth. In the European Union, demand for high-skilled employees will rise by more than 3.5 million as the share of high-skilled jobs increases from 29% in 2010 to about 35% in 2020. The share of middle-skilled jobs will remain steady at about 50%. But the share of jobs for the low-skilled will drop from 20% in 2010 to less than 15% in 2020. [29]

The US Bureau of Labor estimates that the number of total jobs for middle-skilled people will grow 11% from 2006 to 2016, while those for high-skilled individuals will grow 15% and those for low-skilled will grow only 8%.[30]

But the missing link in the discussion is the fact that a growing percentage of traditionally low-skilled jobs now require basic digital literacy and fundamental information-processing skills. To put it another way, they are becoming more middle-skilled. The availability of jobs for the truly unskilled is likely to see an even more severe decline than the forecasters say.

Innovation is the core of the economy you live in, and is being fueled by ICT as a fire is transformed into an inferno by a rush of oxygen. Innovation is becoming almost exclusively a game for the skilled, who can add value to everything they touch during the workday. If you accept those ideas, then you can appreciate the need to ensure that your community experiences "brain gain" rather than "brain drain." In this complex century, we face so many challenges, from the economic and financial to the social and environmental, that we are all tempted to stand stunned, like the proverbial deer in the headlights, while doom rushes down upon us. Life forces us to choose which challenges we will give our attention to. For the future of the local community, no issue is of greater importance than making sure you are on the right side of the gain/drain divide.

CHAPTER THREE

The Three Sides of Innovation

One evening in 1969, the city of Chattanooga, Tennessee received the kind of publicity that any city would prefer to do without. The iconic television news anchor Walter Cronkite reported that Chattanooga had just been named by the US Department of Health, Education and Welfare as the city with the worst air pollution in America.

It could not have come as a surprise to the good people of Chattanooga. The city's prosperity had long been based on industrial foundries – factories that melt metal into a liquid, pour it into moulds and produce cast-metal parts in iron, aluminium, bronze and other materials. They are the very definition of heavy industry, all blazing furnaces, showering sparks and belching smokestacks, and Chattanooga had long done all it could to attract, grow and retain the business.

Geography was not Chattanooga's friend in this regard. It lies in a valley encircled by mountains. Cold air tends to flow over those mountains into the valley and become trapped in what metcorologists call a temperature inversion, so that the output of those smokestacks stayed where it was.

Chattanooga's citizens had grown used to having to turn on the headlights of their cars at midday in order to see. Businessmen learned to take an extra shirt to the office so that they could change out of the dirt-pocked one they had started out the day wearing. Sure the city was gritty, but it was wealthy and proud – until Uncle Walter made it a poster child for the worst excesses of industry operating without regard for its impact on the community around it.

The 1969 newscast marked a turning point for the city. A group of citizens and local government assembled to develop a new vision of an economy that could prosper without condemning its people to lung disease. Spurred by a sense of crisis, it succeeded in forging a partnership with the private sector, which was used to making decisions on its own. A campaign by the Chattanooga Chamber of Commerce led to approval of an Air Pollution Control Ordinance, which created an Air Pollution Control Board and set restrictions on almost all pollution-causing activities in Hamilton County, of which Chattanooga is the seat. The deadline for achieving clean-air goals was set for October 14, 1972 and, incredibly, every major pollution source in the county was in compliance by that date, at a cost of over $40 million.[31]

The campaign to clear the air did not aim to create a precedent, but that is precisely what it did. A process of community "visioning" – uniting business and government – had worked. Why stop there? The community continued to envision a new future, and it led to revitalization of the downtown core and the construction of a new waterfront with America's largest freshwater aquarium as a major tourist attraction. It led to today's focus on brain gain: retaining the talent that issues from the University of Tennessee and Chattanooga State Technical and Community College.

In 2012, it led Chattanooga to declare itself a Gig City based on the fiber-to-the-premise network built by its municipal electric utility. A Gig University project aimed to attract entrepreneurs and students to develop plans for businesses that could make use of the enormous capacity of the network. Working through its Chamber of Commerce, Chattanooga became one of ICF's Top7 Intelligent Communities and attracted the likes of a Volkswagen assembly plant, an IBM simulation center, an Amazon.com distribution center and Blue Cross Blue Shield insurance.

Adding Another Angle

Chattanooga is one of many communities where cooperation between government and business has created progress. The Waterloo Region, known as Canada's Technology Triangle for the three cities that anchor it, is another. But the reference to a three-sided bit of geometry is more than purely geographic.

The entrepreneurial ecosystem that underlies its success has many sources, but none is quite as central or seminal as the University of Waterloo. Because of its engineering programs, the Waterloo Region has become renowned for businesses that require precision engineering, and has attracted the only Lexus plant that Toyota operates outside Japan, as well as a host of home-grown technology players. Research institutes abound, including the Waterloo Centre for Automotive Research and the Centre for International Governance Innovation. Each is more than an academic organization, just as the University of Waterloo has never been a purely scholarly place. Instead, they represent the third side of the Technology Triangle: business, government and universities collaborating to generate innovation, economic growth and local solutions to problems both local and global.

Whether it is called an Innovation Triangle, the Triple Helix or a Public-Private Partnership, the triangle represents an understanding that the 21st Century is no place for organizations to go it alone. The pace of disruptive change is too fast and the variables in the innovation equation are too many for a single organization to cover all the ground. Businesses, both manufacturers and investors, need the ideas and data generated by researchers and educators who work at the leading edge of what is possible. Those researchers and educators benefit professionally from understanding what is commercially feasible and personally from the opportunity to profit from technologies they create in the laboratory.

The participation of local government serves a different purpose. It helps to create infrastructure and an ecosystem where innovation-driven businesses can flourish, by rallying the community and building a specific vision of the future. Through smart policies, it helps to maintain and grow the supply of talent that business requires. And by representing the public interest, it helps ensure that more of the benefits of innovation accrue to the place it happens, while minimizing the downsides of success.

In a Silicon Valley, we see business and academia intersect, giving rise to one of the most fertile technology centers on earth. But the ethos of the Valley has long been that the best role for government is to stay out of the way. The result has been sprawl, transportation snarls, high and booming levels of income inequality and other quality of life problems. Having nearly exhausted the capacity of the Valley, the tech wave has rolled north to San Francisco, where citizens are now complaining of the same set of ills. It is hardly a catastrophe – no dark cloud of smog that dirties shirts and makes headlines – but the more active involvement of local government can help quality of life and economic success to run in tandem rather than fight for dominance.

Not that managing a three-side relationship among such different partners is easy. When government dominates, it tends to stifle innovation. When businesses operate without input from government and citizens, the benefits tend to bypass the community while such bad by-products as pollution or soaring living costs stay local. When educational institutions fail to fit into the mix, everyone loses.

It is human nature to operate in silos, because we know our own business best and prefer that others keep their noses out of it. But Intelligent Communities recognize that the path to prosperity leads in a more challenging direction: through intensive, sometimes contentious collaboration among government, business and the institutions that represent education, culture and citizen interests.

Collaboration is a simple-sounding word with a vast meaning. It is not simply cooperation, which is more often a non-aggression pact than a search for a win-win solution. Collaboration runs deeper. It is built on a foundation of trust, that scarcest of resources. It is the ability to work far beyond the normal boundaries of our organizations while simultaneously meeting the demands those organizations place on us.

How does such collaboration get started? According to Rashik Parmar, President of the IBM Academy of Technology, the Innovation Triangle usually begins with a problem that a lot of people care about.

It may be air pollution, as in the case of Chattanooga, or economic stagnation. It could be brain drain or the loss of cultural heritage or lack of broadband connectivity. It may be an opportunity, instead: to host an international event, to win a prize, or attract a cultural icon. It does not matter much where it originates or even what it is. What matters is that so many people take it personally and consider it urgent that they create the potential for broad collaboration.

A cause that people care about generates the energy needed to create a movement, with excited people, powerful slogans and banners waving in the breeze. It makes possible the next step, which is to begin engaging the three sides of the triangle in creating a roadmap for the future.

And that is when, very often, the breeze seems to die and the waving banners fall limp. From lofty ideas and blazing enthusiasm, things turn to paralysis. Or so it seems.

As multiple organizations engage, says to Dr. Parmar, there follows an inevitable jockeying for leadership. Time is eaten up. Everyone agrees on the need to do something, but everyone balks at the idea of being the first to share potentially lucrative ideas or contribute resources. Energetic efforts to forge progress appear to lead nowhere.

What is really going on, however, is that the various organizations are slowly building trust in each other. Personal relationships are being created that gradually open pathways for sharing among organizations. It is only when such trust is established that progress becomes possible.

It speeds things up if the parties understand what is going on: if they focus consciously on defining what each party will give and what each party hopes to get. But there is only so fast it can proceed.

What counts is perseverance. Perseverance, in turn, can be fed by an effort to create small victories: an alliance here, a positive bit of news there – anything to keep the parties at the table to do the hard work of building trust.

Innovation Triangles tend to succeed, says Parmar, when they create a compelling and specific vision of the future – one that addresses the burning issue that kicked off the effort in the first place – and where one or more leaders have both the trust and the personal drive to produce results.

Trust in Action
A remarkable example of trust in action can be found in Oulu, Finland, where the formation of the Innovation Triangle dates back to the 1980s. Today, the city of 188,000 is served by an open and free Wi-Fi network called panOULU. It represents

collaboration among the City of Oulu, the University of Oulu, the Oulu University of Applied Sciences and the incumbent ISP. They reached agreement to pool their 1,300 individual Wi-Fi access points into one network with a single sign-on. The business model is sustained by sales of panOULU subscriptions to companies that install access points on their premises and instantly gain access to a network used citywide It sounds simple – but such cross-sector networking is extremely rare, because it requires each party to surrender sole control of what it views as a vital asset.

The panOULU network is actually a fairly modest example of the Innovation Triangle, which is estimated to generate 75% of the region's ICT-based economy. In Oulu, the base of the triangle, supporting all the rest, is the academic sector. The University of Oulu, Oulu University of Applied Sciences and the local office of VT, Finland's national R&D lab, have developed multiple long-term projects investigating fields with strong commercial potential, from wireless technologies to digital healthcare and the future of the internet. Established companies participate eagerly and about 400 new companies are formed each year to try their hand at commercializing research. These relationships are formalized in the Oulu Innovation Alliance (OIA), which works to provide a "one-stop shop" approach promoting innovation, research, development, testing and commercialization.

In Taichung, Taiwan, the base of the Triangle is government, led for nearly fifteen years by Mayor Jason Hu. He and his team seized the opportunity created by amalgamation of the surrounding county into the city – a change mandated by national government – to form a sprawling metropolis of 2.6 million people. With the political change came large-scale investment of public money in infrastructure. Mayor Hu's team leveraged this through relationships with communications carriers and transit companies to expand blazing-fast broadband and create intelligent transportation systems to tie together the urban core and rural outliers. Mayor Hu, a larger than life personality, has acted the grand maestro throughout, weaving culture and industry, commercialization and government, transportation and high speed broadband into a symphony called the Intelligent Community of Taichung. This is a community that has demonstrated to the world how – by developing and promoting new ideas in an ecosystem of positive thought leadership – a city far from the nation's capital in the north can become the poster child of a movement.

The other sides of the Triangle are ably represented in Taichung. It is home to 13 universities, of which the largest is Feng Chia University with 21,000 students. Feng Chia alone has launched more than 40 research institutes, which are funded through a mix of government contracts and private-sector projects that motivate close collaboration with business. Working with business partners, Taichung has turned unproductive city-owned lands into massive science parks, including the unique Precision Machinery Industrial Technology Park with its Surface Grinding Machine Training center, shared by all of the industries in the sector. Another example of collaborative innovation is the GIS Faculty at Feng Chia University, which worked with the city's urban planners and scientists to develop the largest GIS Institute in Asia with over 150 full time staff working on projects from developing hundreds of layers of mapping including unique 3D applications to remote sensors, unmanned vehicles and helicopters that constantly monitor the weather and land-flow conditions in Taiwan.

When the Innovation Triangle succeeds, it becomes increasingly hard to tell – and increasingly less important to know – which of the partners is most critical to its success. An example is the MaRS Discovery District in downtown Toronto. It is a major real estate development, start-up incubator and business accelerator all in one, developed by a public-private partnership. Collaborators include provincial entities like the Ontario Network of Excellence and Ontario Ministry of Innovation, as well as surrounding hospitals and foundations, companies housed in the MaRS complex and institutions like the Ontario College of Art and Design, Ryerson University and University of Toronto. It captures the commercial potential of Toronto's $1 billion in annual science and technology research spending, providing a sustainable innovation pipeline for the Discovery District organizations but also beyond into the greater Toronto region. At the core of MaRS is a collaborative, interdisciplinary and cross-industry hub within a unique architectural environment that lends itself to chance discovery and collaboration by means of access to market research, entrepreneurship-focused events, workshops and related programming to help entrepreneurs succeed.

Breaking Out
But innovation ecosystems don't have to remain within a single geographic boundary. The Ontario Technology Corridor is a unique partnership of the cities of Ottawa, Toronto and Waterloo, along with the Province of Ontario, that works with private sector entities to promote the corridor to international markets. Likewise the eleven top cities across Canada formed a collaboration called Consider Canada's City Alliance, promoting the nation's business sectors and

undertaking meetings abroad to attract investment, talent and job creation.

One of the most intriguing collaboration models currently being developed is a Global Innovation Triangle created through the efforts of the Intelligent Communities of Eindhoven in the Netherlands, Waterloo and Taipei, Taiwan. All three communities see the benefit of sharing information and learning more about each other's communities, industry sectors and talent pool. Dollars-and-cents opportunities are even more enticing: to gain proficiency in new industries, to create international joint ventures for their companies, and to provide each other's businesses with market entry. If creating an Innovation Triangle at the local level is difficult, forging one that bridges the Atlantic and Pacific Oceans represents a major challenge – but also an innovation with huge potential for other cities around the world.

Key to the success of these local, regional and international initiatives is the partnership that the municipalities have with the private sector and the institutions in each of their communities. Business clearly wants to meet with business in a B2B setting; institutions can partner with other institutions to share in research and student exchanges; and governments can learn best practices from each other. But it is only when they work in harmony that they can tap the potential of the Innovation Triangle. Collaboration on this scale is not a game for the faint of heart – but it is fast becoming fundamental to community growth and prosperity in our complex, hyper-competitive century.

CHAPTER FOUR

Standing in the Middle

In the global economy of today, where too much information ripples across the planet at light speed, things are often not what they seem.

Open any mainstream newspaper or magazine that covers business news, and you will find the pages or their digital equivalents filled with stories of companies of inter-galactic size: Royal Dutch Shell, Walmart and China National Petroleum, all with sales well north of $400 billion; Toyota and Volkswagen reporting about $250bn; Samsung at $180bn, and Apple and Gazprom at a piddling $150bn or so.

Yet when it comes to the local economy, where most of us live and earn our livings, the giants are not where the action is. In Europe, 99% of all businesses are small-to-midsize (SME). They provide two-thirds of all private-sector jobs and create more than half of the total value in the economy.[32]

In the US, SMEs make up all but 0.3% of private-sector employers and provide half of private-sector employment. More importantly, they contribute nearly one-third of all *new* private-sector jobs and make up a remarkable 98% of all companies involved in export.[33] SMEs are not as dominant in the economies of poor nations, where they account on average for only 17% of economic activity and one-third of new jobs.[34] But in an emerging market nation like Brazil, SMEs already make up close to 100% of all private-sector companies and employ 68% of the workforce.[35]

Not the picture you carry around in your head, is it? The Galactic Overlords have a lot of scale and a lot of clout, but the SMEs are what touch our lives.

This misalignment between reality and belief may help explain why as much as 80% of the resources of a typical economic development marketing budget go to attracting businesses from outside the region, while 80% of economic growth typically emerges from companies already there.[36]

This is not to suggest that the small businesses of your city or region are powerhouses of job growth. The majority of small businesses stay small. They are created by people who prefer to be their own bosses rather than work for an employer, and their principle aim is to replace the income that the owner would otherwise get from a salary If they employ a half-dozen or half-hundred people, they are doing well indeed. The average SME in Australia employs 3.5 people.[37] In Canada, the average is 7.1.[38] According to research from MIT's David Birch, only 4% of *all* US companies are what he termed "gazelles" – firms that double their sales every four years and are responsible, in his calculations, for 70% of all new jobs.[39] These are the companies to which every community would like to offer a home, but they are a rare breed everywhere.

That is why savvy economic developers strike a more equal balance between attracting outside investment and identifying and nurturing their own gazelles. One of the authors of this book played a role in attracting a single executive of an Indian company, Tech Mahindra, to the Greater Toronto Area in the mid-2000s – and the firm now employs more than 2,000 people in the region. But he works today in the technology start-up capital of Canada, the city of Waterloo, where both BlackBerry and OpenText are still headquartered and there is no end in sight to innovation.

Learning from the *Mittelstand*

There are places in the world where SMEs are the backbone of the economy, where they contribute solid and sometimes sizzling growth. The best known is Germany, where the *Mittelstand* – about 3.5 million small-to-midsize, family-owned firms – has powered a strong recovery from the financial crisis. *Mittelstand* companies make up nearly 80% of private-sector employment in Germany and 98% of the country's 350,000 exporters. In the first quarter of 2011, Germany's economy grew at a 6.1% annualized rate and posted unemployment figures that hit a 20-year low. *Mittelstand* companies are estimated to be growing at 12% per year, which is the kind of rate found in China, Brazil and other emerging markets [40]

How do they do it?

Part of the *Mittelstand*'s success stems from specialization. The sector is dominated by companies that make things critical to industrial processes: pumps, nozzles, high-temperature furnaces, measuring equipment and metal stamping machinery. Buyers tend to value extreme precision and high quality over price, which helps defend *Mittelstand* companies from direct competition with lower-cost, lower-quality manufacturers in developing nations. Germany is a high-cost place to manufacture anything, and its companies can only succeed if customers see a value in its products and services that justifies the resulting higher price.

Linn High Therm GmbH manufactures high-temperature industrial and laboratory furnaces. It was founded in 1969 by Horst Linn, using a small loan, in a 550-square-foot rented workshop. His first success was with furnaces used to cast dental crowns and cavity fillings, but the company long ago left that market when it was flooded by cheaper products. In search of profitable niches, Linn has expanded into – among other things – furnaces for making fluorescent materials that go into energy-saving light bulbs and anti-counterfeiting measures on bank notes. The company has never abandoned its commitment to high-priced high performance: its 125 employees have generated 90 registered patents since the company's founding.[41]

But specialization is only the most obvious contributor to the success of the German companies standing proudly in the middle of the economy. The specialization, the precision and the patents are the product of an ecosystem that the *Mittelstand* companies inhabit. It is another example of the Innovation Triangle: an ecosystem that fosters continuous innovation to drive quality higher, push costs lower, introduce new methods and open new markets.

The ecosystem includes, in addition to the companies themselves, universities and technical schools that work hand-in-glove with researchers and engineers at the companies. The small number of large, name-brand firms, from Siemens to Volkswagen, is surrounded by tiers of midsize suppliers, and these in turn are served by a network of smaller suppliers. Being relatively small, *Mittelstand* companies have fewer barriers between management and workers, which tends to improve cooperation and ensure that ideas flow freely.[42]

Government does its part as well. The best-known example is a national program called *Kurzarbeit*, meaning "short work." In most countries, when recession strikes, companies lay off employees to match shrinking demand for their products or services. When the recession slammed Germany in 2008, the national government subsidized companies that cut hours rather than staff. The financial support, plus a lot of belt-tightening, allowed SMEs to retain skilled staff, which in turn permitted the companies to seize growth opportunities when the recession eased its grip. In 2010, according to a survey by the Ifo Institute in Munich, 22% of all Germany firms and 34% of manufacturers were still taking advantage of the program.[43]

Kirsten Schoder-Steinmüller, who runs Schoder GmbH, took advantage of *Kurzarbeit* when a single client cancelled a large number of orders for the metal face plates and high-tech engraving tools her company manufactures. With the help of the program – as well as by suspending a profit-sharing program, cutting overhead and tapping company reserves – she was able to retain her 70-person staff until business picked up again.

As an example of smart, precisely targeted government policy, *Kurzarbeit* is hard to beat. But Germany is hardly the only place where innovation ecosystems have taken root. Cities and regions in many places have worked with skill and patience to craft the kind of business-university-government Triangle that is the foundation of the *Mittelstand*. Unlike efforts to create Silicon Whatevers – the ill-fated attempts to recreate the organic success of Silicon Valley – these Intelligent Communities have set up the three-sided ecosystems within their own unique cultures and to exploit their own unique competitive advantages.

"Take an Extra $25. New York is an Expensive Place."

Those words of wisdom came from the City Council of Stratford, Ontario, Canada, in 1952. A prominent citizen, journalist Tom Patterson, had come before the Council with a proposal. Patterson wanted to travel, at Council's expense, to New York City, where he would somehow convince legendary British director Tyrone Guthrie to come to his city and found a summer Shakespeare Festival in the park. His pitch? Who could resist attending Shakespeare in the park on the banks of the Avon River in a town called Stratford?

These were hard times in Stratford. Its prosperity had been built on agriculture and on serving as a repair depot for the steam engines of the Canadian National (CN) railway. Agriculture was still going strong – though employing fewer people every year – but a decision by CN management had centralized repair services somewhere else on the line. No idea promoting the community's survival was too crazy to consider. And so, on January 22, the Council signed off on Patterson's brainstorm, giving him $25 more than he had originally requested for the trip.

Patterson did meet with the legendary Tyrone. More than once, as a matter of fact, which required more $125 disbursements by Council. But by July of the following year, the Stratford Shakespeare Festival, under artistic director Guthrie, presented its inaugural performance of *Richard III*, starring Alec Guinness, under a massive tent in the park.

That moment in time made cultural tourism a new industry in Stratford. It was truly a home-grown economic development solution, and the first sign of a new innovation ecosystem in the making. But six decades would pass before the next sign appeared.

During that time, the Festival thrived. By 2010, it was the largest employer in the city and generated C$135 million in local economic activity and C$70 million in tax revenue for all levels of government. Stratford grew with it, reaching a population of 32,000. But the Festival, restaurants and lodging were seasonal businesses that brought prosperity only four months of the year.

Then, in 2003, the people of Stratford elected Dan Mathieson as their Mayor. He was a young, entrepreneurial businessman with deep roots in the city, and he set out to change the way Stratford did business.

His first priority was to embrace high-speed broadband connectivity and take it to heights that a small Canadian community like his had never done before. He believed that broadband needed to be treated as basic infrastructure, not a luxury amenity. As he told *The Globe and Mail* in August 2013, "In the future economy, the data that flows across those networks is going to become part of everyday life, if it hasn't already. If you can't entice commercial entities to do it, then government should look at how they can play a role in advancing public broadband." [44]

His vision led to a series of strategic choices. Like many rural cities, Stratford owned its own municipal electric utility. In the 1990s, the utility had laid optical fiber along its rights of way to provide communications capacity for lease to large industrial customers. Early in his tenure, Mayor Mathieson faced pressure from Ontario Province to privatize the utility, supposedly in the name of efficiency. His Council chose a different path. It spun the utility off into a pair of private companies with the city as sole shareholder: a hydro company to own and operate the electrical system and a services company to become a data utility that operated the dark fiber.

By 2012, the services company had grown its network to 60 km (37 mi) and introduced 1 Gbps connections to 125 locations including city facilities and schools. The network also served as the backbone of a 300-node Wi-Fi network, which the hydro company used to roll out a smart meter program to 18,000 customers.

What Mayor Mathieson and his team were creating was a new innovation ecosystem, built on home-grown talent but proving equally attractive to external investment. Today Stratford is leveraging that ecosystem to transform its economy. The fiber network proved pivotal in attracting external investment from the Royal Bank of Canada, which built a national data centre in the area. The city-owned utility has signed an agreement with a private carrier to provide retail triple-play services over its network as well as extending fiber to premises throughout the city. The network has already enabled the Stratford Shakespeare Festival to significantly improve its web-based services and expand online marketing across North America.

City Council and the local business community created a Stratford Tourism Alliance, which launched online and traditional advertising campaigns to make Stratford a destination for "foodies" and cultural tourists. In its first year, the web traffic grew 200% while Ontario Tourism's traffic fell 18% in response to recession. More than half of all leisure travelers carry smartphones, and the Alliance introduced a mobile site in 2010 and mobile versions of its "Savor Stratford" foodies and Festival campaigns. Apps for the iPhone, iPad, Android and BlackBerry followed in 2011, which provided everything from reservations for hotels and restaurants to schedules of events and augmented reality. Online, the many individual private businesses of Stratford's tourism industry were now acting as one, with all of the advantages of scale usually enjoyed by much bigger companies.

With each addition to Stratford's ecosystem, the city's attractiveness to innovators has increased. The Mayor's team has successfully sold Stratford as a test bed for technology projects – a city large enough to give new technologies a meaningful test but easy to operate in due to its small size. Toshiba, Cisco, BlackBerry, Inter-Op and Clemson University all have pilots running in Stratford. These international brand names lend validation to a strategy that has proven its value to the city. During the financial crisis, the near-crash of the North American auto industry pushed unemployment in

Stratford to record highs as the city lost 1,600 mostly low-skilled jobs in manufacturing. During the same period, the city gained 700 high-paying jobs requiring ICT skills and within three years found itself managing a new problem: a labor shortage.

Pedal to the Metal

Just down the road from Stratford, Kurtis McBride stood proudly as he waited to receive his graduation certificate from the President of the University of Waterloo at the Waterloo Accelerator Centre. As a kid, Kurtis had spent summers sitting in a lawn chair on a baking-hot Toronto street corner, counting traffic for his father's transportation management consulting firm and thinking that there had to be a better way to do it.

He turned out to be right. Years later, the company he helped found, Miovision, provides traffic data collection and management solutions for 450 customers in 30 countries. It got its start at the University of Waterloo, an institution founded in 1957 by two businessmen and a Catholic university president, who wanted this new university to help give the next generation of business leaders a strong start. It was they who set the university's unusual intellectual property (IP) policy: it grants students and faculty who create IP, whether technology or a business idea, all rights to their innovation. No licensing, no revenue sharing, nothing.

Founded in 2005, Miovision was the first graduate of Waterloo's Accelerator Centre in 2009. Since then, the Centre has built a global reputation for the cultivation of technology entrepreneurship and the creation and acceleration of new technology companies. But it has also gone beyond the usual boundaries of a university accelerator, with an impact on the entire Waterloo region.

At any given time, the Centre is home to about 50 start-up companies that use its office space and the services of advisors and mentors, who provide management education, legal counsel and financial guidance. It also houses offices of partner institutions, including the National Research Council, the University's tech transfer and commercialization office and Communitech, a nonprofit founded by Waterloo entrepreneurs to drive commercialization of innovative technologies. These organizations extend the Accelerator Centre's influence throughout the region, which goes by the name Canada's Technology Triangle.

Communitech, for example, operates another hub in nearby Kitchener in a brick-and-beam former tannery complex. It has become a second beehive of activity with hundreds of start-ups surrounded by such major tech players as Google, Desire2Learn, Agfa and Christie Digital. More conventional businesses, like the retailer Canadian Tire, have offices there to tap the expertise and innovation of new companies.

On average around the world, 45% of start-ups are still around five years after their founding. In Waterloo's rich ecosystem, the current average is 85%.

The University's intellectual property policy is a kind of gamble, a bold bet that the university will benefit more by freeing its alumni to succeed than by placing a claim on their future earnings. That bet has paid off handsomely. The most successful start-ups emerging from U Waterloo have stayed where they were founded – from BlackBerry to OpenText – and the entrepreneurs at their head have ploughed money into enriching the ecosystem that helped them succeed. Waterloo is now home to 150 institutes and think tanks founded by Waterloo alumni, from the Mike and Opheia Lazaridis Quantum-Nano Centre to the prestigious Perimeter Institute for Theoretical Physics. Since 2007, when ICF recognized Waterloo as its Intelligent Community of the Year, its innovation ecosystem has experienced an 8-fold increase in new company creation.

The result of all this interaction – both formally structured and as off-the-cuff as an evening conversation over beer and pizza – is an Innovation Triangle that has helped to create nearly 1,100 tech companies employing more than 30,000 people and generating $30 billion in annual revenue. This, in a city of 550,000 people. Despite the well-publicized fall of BlackBerry, the Waterloo economy continues to generate two new home-grown tech starts every day of the year. Technology companies large and small also continue to move in, partly to recruit BlackBerry's talent but mostly to benefit from the long-established Triangle of business, government and education. Google, Motorola Mobility, Twitter, Cisco, Square are some of the new and established tech companies opening offices there in recent years.

"The area has a really strong density of tech talent," Bryan Power, the talent director for Square, told *The New York Times*. His company planned to have about 40 employees working in the region by the end of 2014. "We have a long timeline for here. We really want to be part of this community."[45]

Information technology is not the whole story, either. Sectors range from advanced manufacturing in automotive tech and food processing to clean tech, financial services and life sciences. And, since 2009, traffic data management solutions from Miovision. Kurtis McBride recognized the value of the innovation ecosystem of Waterloo, and positioned his new company to make the most of it.

What to Do When the Boom Ends

Tallinn, the capital of Estonia and a Top7 Intelligent Community of 2013, has had a storybook history in the 21st Century. After 50 years of Soviet rule, in 1991, it achieved the first true independence in national memory. Only 14 years later, in 2005, a writer for *The New York Times* called it "a sort of Silicon Valley on the Baltic Sea."

What happened? In the best tradition of economic booms, government policy and hot money combined to produce a remarkable if short-lived result.

Decisions by national government liberalized both banking and telecommunications, which allowed foreigners to buy big stakes in banks and telecom carriers, into which they poured substantial investment. Government also identified information technology as a strategic sector and announced a national goal to put a personal computer into every public classroom. Government funding poured into computer hardware and software, jumpstarting an indigenous industry, while private-sector investors doubled down on the traditional boom sectors of real estate and infrastructure. Both kinds of investors tapped the pent-up ambition of businesspeople and technologists to grow beyond the confines of the past.

Tallinn and the nation badly needed such investment after decades of neglect – but it proved far more than the market could absorb. When the financial crisis came in 2008, it hit Estonia and its principal city of Tallinn very hard. Several thousand companies went bankrupt and layoffs, particularly of the low-skilled, rose into the tens of thousands.

While fighting the fires of the recession with such measures as rent subsidies for business and heating subsidies for the unemployed, Tallinn's government, universities and business leaders began planning their second act. Like Stratford and Waterloo, they went about constructing a better innovation ecosystem.

Tallinn has 23 universities and technical schools, more than enough to produce a highly skilled workforce. With the support of the city, the educational establishment has launched multiple incubators targeting creative services, medical and biotech, mechatronics and ICT. The oldest is the TEHNOPOL (Technopol in English) at Tallinn's Science Park, which has leveraged its location near the IT College of Tallinn University to nurture more than 160 home-grown companies employing 3,200 people. More established tech companies cluster at the Ülemiste City industrial estate. The estate is expanding 50% to house 250 companies, making it the Baltics' biggest knowledge-based development.

Europe's first gaming accelerator opened in Tallinn in 2013, and the TEHNOPOL opened a new start-up incubator building in 2012. Estonia's government has added to the mix with a public-private partnership accelerator called Start-Up WiseGuys, and a loose group of entrepreneurs have imitated their peers in Waterloo by starting a private incubator called Garage48 in the very heart of the city.

Technology, however, is not just a game for youth. From 2007 to 2011, the Tallinn Technical University doubled participation in its lifelong learning programs, while the city significantly expanded public access computer sites and training programs for the disenfranchised. These programs help ensure that ICT-based economic development is not just for an elite, better-educated minority, but becomes integral to how Tallinn's citizens live their lives.

In Stratford, Waterloo and Tallinn, they pay their respects to the Galactic Overlords of business that make headlines and command global attention. They even are glad to take their money in the form of foreign direct investment. But they know which side of the bread really provides their butter. For communities large and small, in industrial and emerging economies, the key to sustainable, long-term growth in the Broadband Economy is to cultivate an innovation ecosystem that advances the prospects of small-to-midsize companies eager for a shot at the big leagues. If it brings the world to their door, so much the better.

CHAPTER FIVE
Education for the Next Billion

In the late 19th Century, John Bell journeyed from Northern Ireland to America with his family as part of the great migration of the Irish to the New World. His people were originally Scots, dispatched to Ireland by a long-ago English king in a futile effort to pacify that land, and were one of the successive waves of Scots-Irish to help populate America.

John was fourteen when his family passed through Ellis Island in New York. They made their way to the state of Pennsylvania and the men of the family, including young John, went to work in the coal mines. And that is where, in all probability, he should have worked for the rest of a life made shorter by constant exposure to coal dust. But he was a bright young lad and, at some point in his late adolescence, he managed to become apprenticed to an attorney. He learned his trade, passed the bar and, moving to the neighboring state of New Jersey, married and went into practice. He ended his working days as municipal counsel to the city of Rutherford and president of the National Starch Company.

John was grandfather to one of this book's authors, and his story is remarkable for two reasons. First of all, it is very rare for any American to make such a dramatic advance in income and social class. The nation prides itself on offering opportunity for advancement to all but, in this century, actually has one of the lowest rates of social mobility among rich nations. In 2006, only 11 percent of the children of low-income parents like John's family managed to move into reasonable affluence by the end of their lives. That is lower rate than in any affluent country except Britain and Italy. [46]

But the really startling thing about his story is the apprenticeship to the lawyer. The idea of a modern-day John Bell moving from the coal mines to a law office is all but unimaginable. He would have needed four years at a university – something he was ultimately able to offer his son – and another three at a law school, all at the astronomical prices charged by American institutions of higher learning compared with average incomes.

Today's innovation economy provides disproportionate rewards to workers with high skill levels and punishes those without them. That makes education the single most important factor in economic success (after the social class you were born into) for individuals and the place they make their home. Perhaps because we now put such a premium on it, education is also being challenged as never before.

Demanding Consumers

The challenges begin on the demand side, where educational consumers are raising questions about the value of what they receive. In India, the state of public education has become a national scandal focusing on unqualified teachers in no-show jobs, chaotic administration and endemic corruption. In both India and China, universities are graduating new engineers and business people at mind-numbing rates but there are deep concerns about their basic qualifications and work-readiness, as well as their abilities in the creative problem-solving essential to innovation.

In the US, public schools are under enormous pressure to measure and improve their outcomes. So severe is that pressure that it has led to the first broadly-accepted national curriculum, the Common Core, in a country where local control of public education is a jealously-guarded right. In Western Europe, where national control of education is well-established, universities offering free or very inexpensive education struggle on tight public budgets to attract top talent in the face of competition from US universities funded largely by student tuition.

In developing nations worldwide, governments struggle to extend elementary, secondary and higher education to their citizens in the face of poverty, poor infrastructure, cultural barriers and weak governing institutions. Educators in Afghanistan and Pakistan are sometimes paying with their lives for striving to bring education to villages ruled by gunmen, who quite rightly see it as a long-term threat to their power.

The challenges are nothing new but the urgency to meet them may be greater than any time in the last fifty years. The exciting news is that this urgency for change is intersecting with the other great revolution underway, in information and communications technology, to put new tools into the hands of educational innovators – powerfully disruptive ones that offer huge potential if we can figure out how to use them well.

Headlines are made at the national and international level. Progress happens locally, where innovators can experiment, learn from unexpected consequences, and adapt to achieve success.

The Day Salman Khan Quit His Job

Whether global or local, educational innovators are attacking three challenges, sometimes individually and sometimes all at once.

The first challenge is cost.

Education, as practiced for the past millennium, is not particularly productive. Teaching has always been one of those professions, like medicine or music, in which customers vastly prefer quality to productivity. A teacher can effectively teach only so many students – and much hot air is expended in many places arguing over exactly how many students should be in the average classroom. The university lecture format, with a professor addressing hundreds of students at a time, is about as productive as education gets, and nobody prefers it to a small discussion class.

The problem appeared insoluble until 2004, when Salman Khan began tutoring his cousin, Nadia, in math over the internet. Khan, the son of a Bangladeshi father and Indian mother, was born and raised in New Orleans in the southern USA. After earning three degrees from MIT, he went to work as one of those rocket scientists in the back offices of a hedge fund, concocting ever-more brilliant computerized trading strategies to make off with an ever-larger share of your money.

Nadia prospered and soon other relatives and friends sought Khan's help. So, he decided to pre-record tutorials and distribute them on YouTube. Khan avoided the standard video format – a guy standing in front of a whiteboard – and instead drew concepts and made calculations on a black screen, with only his voice for accompaniment. The videos turned into a viral hit and eventually attracted enough financial support from donors to let Khan leave the hedge fund. One of his supporters, Microsoft founder Bill Gates, said "It was a good day his wife let him quit his job." [47]

Today, the Khan Academy has an online library of more than 4,300 videos on elementary and secondary math as well as computer science, biology and other topics. Having delivered more than 260 million lessons, the Academy is supported by multi-million-dollar donations from foundations and tech companies. The Academy's web site offers, in addition to the videos, progress tracking, practice exercises and tools to help teachers integrate the lessons into their classrooms.

And all of it, from videos to tools, is completely free. Khan describes his long-term goal as providing "tens of thousands of videos in pretty much every subject" to create "the world's first free, world-class virtual school where anyone can learn anything." [48]

It does not take much imagination to see the impact. According to PointTopic, there were more than 640 million fixed broadband subscriptions in mid-2012.[49] Ericsson estimates that the world had 1.1 billion mobile broadband subscriptions at the same point.[50] Even considering overlap – people who have both fixed and mobile subscriptions – there are easily a billion people around the world who can access the Khan Academy – a billion potential classrooms requiring only a broadband connection to join in. That is a revolution deserving of all the headlines it can garner.

The Khan Academy offers more than just an attack on cost. It offers a big advance in the second great challenge facing education today, which is improving quality.

Mathematics and the sciences are particularly difficult topics to teach. In daily life, we practice them much less than verbal skills, so young people seldom come to school with a natural foundation. Both are cumulative disciplines requiring mastery at each step in the learning process. If some of the fundamentals of multiplication elude you in school, you will be completely helpless when it comes to learning long division. If you are fuzzy on the difference between velocity (speed) and acceleration (the rate of change in speed), you are going to be one confused cowboy when it comes time to understand the physics of an object falling to the ground.

The degree of difficulty means that the quality of math and science teaching varies dramatically, and the time pressure exerted by the curriculum means that struggling students are often left behind. An author of this book remembers intervening when his bright young daughter began floundering in an elementary school math class. She had failed to grasp one or two key concepts and her teacher seemed to have little idea how to identify the missing links. Extracurricular practice with Dad solved the problem, not to mention giving Dad a chance to refresh his own math skills.

An October 2012 study from the University of Chicago reported that mathematics anxiety (a term that generates 8.1 million hits on Google) prompts a response in the brain similar to that of a person experiencing physical pain.[51]

Effective online instruction, thoughtfully divided into short segments focusing on a specific progression of skills, can be the antidote to this torture. Students can review a concept as many times as it takes for them to understand it. Using Khan Academy's chat system, they can see questions that other students had about it and pose their own. They can practice the skill until they achieve mastery and mark their progress online. And they can do it without the humiliation of feeling stupid in front of a jury of their peers.

The Year of the MOOC

These quality improvements are the reason that *The New York Times* named 2012 "The Year of the MOOC." MOOC stands for Massively Open Online Course. The world's first MOOC was Britain's UKeU, which offered university courses online beginning in 2003 but was shut down a year later. The publicly-funded project had cost £50m but attracted only 900 students. But it proved to be only slightly ahead of its time.[52] By 2007, Advanced Learning Interactive Systems Online (ALISON) had launched with five basic education courses and no students, but survived to deliver 60 million lessons through the end of 2012.[53]

The term MOOC was not coined until 2008, however, to describe a course taken by 25 tuition-paying students at the University of Manitoba in Canada, as well as 2,300 other students from the general public who took the course free of charge. The course content was available through web video, RSS feeds, online discussions, blog posts and even Second Life.

This set the pattern for MOOCs to come, which are best thought of as the Khan Academy with a lot more bells and whistles, applied to higher education.

"The Year of the MOOC" designation arose because 2012 was the year when three privately-funded US MOOC companies – Udacity, Coursera and edXed – were founded to commercialize courses delivered by top professors at major US universities, from Stanford and Princeton to MIT and Harvard. They began attracting enrollments exceeding 100,000 students per course. The University of New South Wales launched Australia's first MOOC in October 2012. By the end of the year, the UK was back in the game with FutureLearn, the Universidad Politécnica de Madrid launched the first Spanish-language MOOC, and Galileo University created Latin America's first MOOC, designed to run on iPhone and iPad.

The MOOCs of 2012 and earlier years fed a basic hunger for learning from students around the world. In 2013, MOOCs began experimenting with offering courses for academic credit. Udacity, in collaboration with San Jose State University in California, was first out of the gate. By May, Udacity, AT&T and the Georgia Institute of Technology had introduced a MOOC-based Master's Degree costing $7,000, a small fraction of the price of a similar degree at a brick-and-mortar institution. [54]

At this early stage, what we *don't* know about MOOCs far outweighs what we *do* know. For example, there seems to be a flaw in the model, for all of its popularity. Enrollment figures are massive – but completion rates are not. According to a 2013 study by Open University Ph.D. student Katy Jordan, the average completion rate is less than 7 percent. The best performer was a computer programming course from Switzerland's École Polytechnique Fédérale de Lausanne, offered on the MOOC platform Coursera, which 19 percent of the 50,000 students who started the course actually finished. The worst performer was a world history course from Princeton University, also on Coursera; of the 83,000 students who signed up, fewer than 1% made it to the finish line. [55]

One of America's most publicized MOOC experiments, at San Jose State University in California, was announced with great fanfare in January 2013 and was suspended in July, when it was found to produce much worse performance than traditional classrooms.[56]

Educators at the elementary, secondary and university levels are also profoundly concerned about how online education integrates into the classroom. Part of that concern is for their own survival. The popularity of MOOCs is forcing universities to reassess the costly business model that requires the physical presence of students and professors on campus. Public school teachers fear that software and hardware will do to them what it has already done to hundreds of thousands of assembly line workers.

But self-interest aside, there is the profound question of what online instruction is good for, what live teaching is good for, and how the two should be interwoven to deliver the highest quality at the lowest cost per student.

"To all those people who declared our experiment a failure," wrote Sebastian Thrun, founder of Udacity, which created San Jose State's MOOC content, "you have to understand how innovation works. Few ideas work on the first try. Iteration is the key. I care about education for everyone, not just the elite. We want to bring high-quality education to everyone, and set up everyone for success."[57]

If MOOCs can actually boost educational productivity – teaching more students better for less money – it will be one of the most profound forces for good in the so-often-sorry history of the human race. It will make it possible to deliver more broadly than ever before the lifelong education that employees, employers and entrepreneurs so desperately need. Distressed urban school districts, remote rural community colleges, factory campuses in the export hot-spots of developing nations – all will have the ability to access the world's best educational content: content, moreover, whose delivery has been refined and improved through interactions with hundreds of thousands of students.

Innovative educators are already testing new ideas. Some are as simple as assigning students with specific gaps in their learning to engage with Khan-Academy-style content online until they get past their problem. Others, like "flipping the classroom," are more far-reaching. In the traditional model, a teacher spends most of a class delivering information, one-to-many, and devotes much less time to working with individuals and small groups on practice, discussion and problem-solving. Teachers flip the classroom when they assign students to watch the lecture part of the class online the day before and devote the entire class to helping students grasp the material, practice using it and achieve individual mastery.

It will be some time before online education matures enough for us to assess its value – and probably equally long before classroom educators stop fearing it. While issues of cost and quality continue to be thrashed out, however, there is a third and equally major challenge being explored at the local level.

Flipping the School

Oulu, Finland is the home of a remarkable educational experiment that turns not just the classroom but the entire school on its head. The school in this case is the Ritaharju Community Center, which provides day care, kindergarten, primary and secondary school classes to about 800 students. It is also a senior center and a youth center, where children from seven to seventeen can spend their free time before and after school in a safe environment – playing, watching TV, doing handcrafts or engaging in that universal pursuit of youth, just hanging out. Though utterly modern, Ritaharju resembles nothing so much as a traditional village, where all ages, genders and temperaments find ways to co-exist, learning important lessons that have nothing to do with the formal curriculum.

But formal curriculum there certainly is. The idea for Ritaharju was born in 2004, when a group of the city's educators were tasked with planning elementary and secondary schools for this fast-growing city. One of their recommendations was the creation of a Smart Schools learning network uniting the city's most innovative schools. Another was the development of an entirely different kind of school, to be located in Ritaharju, a relatively new neighbourhood of about 4,000 people that was proving a magnet for young families with children.

The city adopted both recommendations and, in 2007, went a step farther by enrolling in the Microsoft Partners in Learning program, an international effort to rethink education and identify the most effective ways to use technology in learning. The final piece of the plan fell into place a year later, when the Deputy Mayor named a multi-disciplinary steering group to plan and implement Ritaharju, which opened in 2010. The major players were the city's school department, Microsoft and the University of Oulu's Center for internet Excellence (CIE).

Visit the Ritaharju Community Center today and you find information and communications technology everywhere. Very young children use fixed workstations with access to the school's servers, while beginning in the 3rd grade, every student receives an individual laptop. Microsoft's OneNote and Live@edu systems integrate live and online learning, curriculum management and parent-student-teacher interaction. ICT is even part of recess. Ritaharju is one of several schools with a digital kiosk on the playground: students use it to challenge kids at other schools to one of the many playground games offered by the system.

The Center for internet Excellence (CIE) is a project of the highly respected University of Oulu that aims to create the next generation of web interface, converting the point-and-click workings of today's web to the kind of immersive environment found in video games. CIE is using Ritaharju as a laboratory to develop immersive learning environments and experiment with gamification: adapting the powerful incentive systems that digital game designers have evolved to keep players hooked to the higher goal of education.

For all the high-tech toys, however, the real revolution at Ritaharju is in the design of learning. You see it as soon as you enter. Big airy classrooms are filled with conventional chairs, desks and tables – but also with couches, upholstered armchairs and coffee tables that breathe an air of homeliness. It is a design based on the belief that people learn best in an environment that puts them emotionally at ease. Many classrooms are separated by air-walls which can be opened to bring classes together. Teachers – a select group who have to apply for posting to Ritaharju – have been retrained to work in teams and to guide student exploration rather than just deliver information.

The whole team thing is pretty serious. There is a library team, a teacher team, a day care team, a youth work team and a special-needs assistant team. IT specialists belong to most teams as well. The team leaders form the Board of Ritaharju, so that the communication flows up, down and across the 100 adults who care for about 800 children.

The performance of both students and teachers is care-fully measured, not just by skills and knowledge acquisition but also by social skills and such intangibles as cultural understanding, patience and self-control. The University runs an experimental program designed to teach prevention of violence and bullying by 6-8-year-olds through a positive, family-oriented approach. Teachers give the program a thumbs-up: "When you punish children for acting out, you are rewarding them with attention," says one teacher. "A positive approach turns the situation around."

If all of this strikes you as insufficiently hard-headed, a bit airy-fairy, consider this. For almost all of the past decade, Finland has led the international league tables of education systems, with top-level rankings in the OECD's Program for International Student Assessment (PISA) of 15-year-olds around the world in reading, math and science. Ritaharju should not be confused with a standard Finnish school. But when the Finns come up with something new in education and conclude that it actually works, the rest of us would be well advised to listen.

Education that Fits

The third and perhaps greatest challenge facing education is "fit" – revamping what we teach and how we teach it to fit the needs of the new century instead of the old.

To a greater degree than ever before, educators and parents everywhere agree on one of the oldest maxims in business: that you can only manage what you can measure. In some countries this is old news, but even in places that have long resisted it, a data-driven approach to assessing students, teachers and schools is rising as inexorably as the tide. There will continue to be fights over what the data means and how it should be applied – to decisions about teacher contracts and salaries, for example – but empiricism is winning. As the late Daniel Patrick Moynihan, a four-term U.S. Senator, ambassador, administration official and academic, is said to have put it: you are entitled to your own opinion, but not to your own facts.

Improving educational productivity and making its quality more consistent are challenges of *scale*. Gains are made by finding more efficient and effective ways to deliver learning to larger numbers of students – to finding ways to better educate the next billion. The challenge of fit is different. It is less about the globe than about the place where students will live and work. The fit is to the needs of the new century as they are expressed regionally and locally. And so, the community has become the most powerful laboratory for experimentation in the mysteries of fit.

In Columbus, Ohio, USA, there is a small but remarkable secondary school located on the campus of Ohio State

University (OSU). A $200,000 grant from the Gates Foundation sparked the vision for a specialized school for up to 400 students in grades 9-12 focused on science, technology, engineering and math (STEM). OSU funded the initial three-year-lease on a building for what would become Metro High School, as well as contributing to development of its curriculum. Battelle, a large not-for-profit research and development company headquartered in Columbus, also fronted money and expertise, and the Educational Council, a partnership of the 16 school districts in the county to which Columbus belongs, agreed to operate the school, which is funded by a mix of public and private dollars.

In an economy where employers complain about their inability to find qualified people for demanding manufacturing, technical and service operations, Metro High School offers a revolutionary idea. Forget about what your grade level is supposed to be based on the year you entered kindergarten. Concentrate instead on what you learn. Metro uses a mastery-based curriculum. Students step through a set of learning objectives and only advance to the next one after they demonstrate mastery of the current one. Think of the Khan Academy and its unlimited opportunity for practice, translate it within the four walls of a school with its live instructors and facilities, and you have Metro High.

In its classrooms, students of all ages are mixed together based on their educational progress rather than age. Some students complete all of their requirements in as little as two years while others need the full four. Students making fast progress can take classes at OSU, while a compulsory internship program exposes all students to work experience before they graduate. By the 11th and 12th grades, most students are on the university campus or doing internships, and the average student graduates with one year of university credit.

As with the Ritaharju Community Center, technology is everywhere and absolutely secondary in importance. Every Metro student receives an Apple laptop, which provides access to an enormous range of online learning content. The school runs on a sophisticated learning management system that provides near-real-time feedback to students and parents on achievement. But the real revolution is in the interaction among students and educators. Putting mastery front and center makes transparent and tangible what is so often not. It is an ideal fit for math and science instruction, with its high degree of difficulty. And as expectations of students are completely different, so are the practices of teachers. An air of friendly, sometimes chaotic energy tempered by respect pervades most classrooms. Metro teachers tend to be flexible and multi-functional, teaching biology one moment and fixing the router the next, without concern over work rules. Everyone's eyes appear to be fixed on the prize of gaining knowledge and putting it to good use.

So is Metro High an elite school, drawing from the most desirable students and delivering a high-quality education at high cost? Remarkably, not. Metro is a magnet school, with a lottery-based admission process that draws half from the city of Columbus and half from suburban districts. The ethnic mix is similar to that of the region, with 50% white students, 25 percent black and the remainder from other ethnic backgrounds. Thirty percent receive a free school lunch – indicating low income – and 25 percent are special-needs students. Educational outcomes are high and the overall cost of that education, despite the technology toys, is among the lowest of all the schools in the region.

Easing the Path to Post-Secondary Education

Columbus, the capital of the state of Ohio, deserves to be better known as a hotspot of educational reform. It is the epicenter of an ongoing earthquake in educational practice called the Central Ohio Compact. This is a consortium of K-12 schools, institutions of higher education, business leaders and local and state economic development officials. The Compact's 2013 strategic plan notes that 59 percent of Ohio jobs needed a post-secondary education in 2010 but that only 36 percent of Ohio adults have a post-secondary credential – though metropolitan Columbus residents are better prepared at 44 percent. The Compact's goal is to raise the Ohio average to 60 percent by 2025.

The Compact's strategy has four themes. It seeks to raise student expectations and readiness, make sure that secondary students are university-ready, remove obstacles for adult learners, and improve affordability of higher education. What makes them more than pious wishes is the Compact's successful approach to integrating secondary and post-secondary education. One example is a program partly funded by Honda that enables students to graduate from secondary school with an associate's certificate in automotive technology, which would otherwise require two more years of schooling. Despite the recent near-death experience of US automotive manufacturing, the sector remains a major employer and easing the path from school to work serves the interests of both students and companies.

One of the partners in the Compact, the Columbus State Community College (CSCC), works intensively with health-care, IT, finance, technology and other sectors in central Ohio to smooth the path of its graduates into the job market. For example, CSCC developed training for the logistics industry, a significant employer in the region, which puts adults who have lost jobs in other industries through a certification program in logistics and then supports job placement, with high rates of success. A new bioscience technology program follows the same development model: CSCC began by working with multiple companies to get agreement on a baseline set of skills. The college then produced a program to train students in these areas, and graduates began arriving at the doors of employers with exactly the skills those employers had agreed in advance were needed most.

When an executive at one of its employer-partners noted that his company "hires on hard skills and fires on soft ones," CSCC created a 3-week course teaching personal communication, problem-solving, leadership, teamwork and conflict resolution. It brings the course to employers as well as to secondary schools in the region.

A more complex project focuses on improving how low-income students pursue a college education. In the US, you can enroll in a two-year community college and then, before completing the program, transfer to a four-year institution and receive credit for courses already completed. The result is that you graduate with a university degree for far less money than it would have cost to attend the same university for four years. Given the astronomical cost of higher education in America, that strategy has played a big role in expanding access.

But with this reward comes risk. If you have to drop out of the university before you graduate, not only do you fail to receive the university degree, you also forego the associate's certificate from the two-year college to which your studies may entitle you. After two to three years of effort you are left with nothing but the debts you incurred to pay for that education.

Making matters worse, the students most likely to drop out are from low-income families – frequently the first of that family to attend a college – who face financial setbacks, family medical emergencies, or simply give in to cultural pressures from well-meaning relatives and friends who do not understand their life choice.

That's an unacceptable risk for young people striving for a better life. To reduce it, the Compact is working to unify standards across two-year and four-year institutions. When the project is complete, transferring students will be able to take a test at the end of their first two years and receive, with a passing grade, their associates' certificate from the two-year college, while at the same time continuing their studies at the four-year institution. If circumstances force them from out of the four-year university, they can still carry their associates' certificate into the marketplace.

The Stratford Triangle

Central Ohio has a lot going for it when it comes to education. OSU is a $6 billion institution. So is Battelle, which is headquartered literally across the street from the OSU campus. When such giants focus on a problem, the odds of finding a solution improve. But refitting education for the next generation is not only a game for weighty institutions.

Stratford is a small city of 30,000, which sits at the center of the richest agricultural region in Ontario, Canada. It is best known as the home of the Stratford Shakespeare Festival, a seasonal business that is the city's largest employer in peak season.

By rights, that is all Stratford should be known for. But it has grown a reputation for two other things that tend to distinguish Intelligent Communities: vision and a pronounced talent for making a deal. Deciding that little Stratford needed the same kind of Innovation Triangle as much bigger places,

Mayor Dan Mathieson and the City Council set out to build one nearly from scratch.

The single biggest gap in the Stratford Triangle was education: it is tough to have a university-business-government alliance without a university. But less than an hour down the road was a place called Waterloo, ICF's 2007 Intelligent Community of the Year, which was home to the University of Waterloo (UW). Today, it has Canada's largest engineering faculty and the world's largest post-secondary cooperative education program, and its graduates have founded companies from BlackBerry to OpenText.

Stratford wanted that some of that entrepreneurial energy and, as it turned out, the university wanted something that Stratford had. UW was interested in expanding its offerings in digital media, with a focus on how these fast-changing technologies would transform business and industry. What Stratford had was its Shakespeare Festival: an enterprise that generated large volumes of high-quality content, considered itself in the education as well as entertainment business, and welcomed the idea of involving students in extending its reach into the digital realm.

Several years went into assembling the components of a deal. The city committed to investing C$10 million to revitalize part of an abandoned industrial site in its downtown core. The Province of Ontario matched that investment, as did OpenText, and the Federal government added C$5 million. The new building opened in October 2012 to 98 undergraduate and 19 graduate students working in state-of-the-art digital media labs for graphic design, animation, web development and audio and video editing. Two-thirds of the students were Canadian, with the remainder coming from around the world.

The Bachelor of Global Business and Digital Arts is a four-year undergraduate program that emphasizes project-oriented learning in partnership with private companies and outside institutions, from famous names like OpenText, Google and BlackBerry to small software developers and the Festival. Students work in project teams that deliberately mix artists, business majors and engineers, which forces the start of the collaboration that will shape their entire careers. Every student graduating from the program leaves UW Stratford as a certified project manager.

The city has lost no time in pursuing economic benefit from the new campus. By January 2013, UW Stratford and the local school district announced the launch of a School Within a University program that will bring university-bound secondary school students on campus for technology training and participation in projects. By May, just before UW Stratford ended its first school year, the Stratford Accelerator opened in a nearby building to provide a local home for digital media start-ups.

The digital media focus spread downward as well as outward. Stratford's school district participates in a Canadian program offering High Skills Majors in a range of fields. At Stratford Central High School, enrollment in the digital media and information technology majors is growing fast. In 2011, one digital media instructor organized the DIGIs, Canada's first national digital media awards for secondary school students and showcased 250 entries from four provinces. Dylan Woodley, one of Central High's students, saw his animation "Pancake Island" go viral on the web and receive national and US media attention, while another of Dylan's videos was featured on the web site of the band Coldplay.

In their different ways, Stratford, Columbus and Oulu are tilling the same field. As revolutionaries like Salman Khan and the MOOCs use ICT to blow the doors off our notions of what is possible, these communities are on a quest to discover what is most needed. The scale is local and regional rather than global and the experimentation is less about technology than it is about people. The outcomes – for their own people and all those around the world who can learn from them – show us, not just what education might be, but what it can become.

Brain Gain

CHAPTER SIX

The Center and the Edge

There are two kinds of cities in the world. Actually, that's a ridiculous statement – there are a lot more than two kinds of cities in the world. But work with us here for a moment. Assuming that the world contains two and only two kinds of cities, they are cities at the Center and cities on the Edge.

Cities at the Center are the ones you know best: London and Paris, Rio de Janeiro and Buenos Aires, Cairo and Johannesburg, Beijing and Tokyo and New Delhi. They are Columbus, capital of the state of Ohio and home to more than three-quarters of a million people. They include Taichung with its 2.7 million people at the geographical center of Taiwan; and Toronto, Canada's financial and media capital, where more than 2.6 million people live and work, producing 11% of the nation's GDP.

Cities on the Edge are the ones you never heard of unless you live near them. They are Tuxtla Gutiérrez, in Mexico's southernmost state of Chiapas; Ballarat in Victoria, Australia; Heraklion on the Greek island of Crete; Ichikawa, Japan; and Porto Alegre, Brazil. They include Moncton in the Canadian province of New Brunswick; Tallinn, the political and economic center of Estonia but located on the eastern edge of the European Union, which it joined in 2004; and Taoyuan Metropolis, which produces most of the world's notebook computers but has long been overshadowed by Taiwan's capital city of Taipei on its northeastern border.

Hub, Spoke and Shadow

For most of history, cities at the Center have been junction points where networks converge, as spokes converge on the hub of a wheel: transportation and utilities, people and products, money and power, knowledge and its application. As such, they are primary beneficiaries of the network effect – an idea proposed by the founder of AT&T – which says that the more people and places a network connects to, the greater its value.

For a city at the Center, all other things being equal, that value tends to flow inward, whether in the form of commuters, of capital or of commerce. The Center tends to be the primary source in its region of employment, entertainment, information and political power, which act as magnetic forces drawing inward all manner of economic activity. The surrounding region benefits greatly as well but inevitably stands in the shadow cast outward from the Center.

Cities on the Edge share the challenges of standing in that shadow. Because of the way value flows, they tend to have less control over their economic destiny. They are more likely to send commuters, capital and commerce toward the Center than to be on the receiving end. And they are typically on the wrong end of the most important trade of all: the trade in talent. Talk to the mayor of almost any city on the Edge and you will hear about the problem of brain drain. For talented young residents, there are so clearly other places to be – places with brighter lights and broader horizons, where like-minded people flock in large numbers and where individual initiative receives greater rewards. For businesses and institutions, there are bigger markets, better access and a more innovative environment to be found the closer they move to the Center. Arts and culture tend to flow outward from the Center to the Edge, only rarely making a return trip.

For a long time, Center cities have had things mostly their own way as population has converged relentlessly on them. Sixty-two years ago, New York and Tokyo were the word's only megacities – urban areas with more than 10 million residents. In 2012, there were 23 of them and the UN predicts that by 2025, there will be nine new megacities in Asia, bringing the world total to 37, all but eight of them in the developing world.[58]

In 2008, for the first time in history, more of the world's people lived in cities than outside of them, and 75 percent of rich-world citizens were urbanites.[59] And why not? One of the best-known proponents of cities, Dr. Richard Florida of the University of Toronto, saw nothing but upside in a 2011 article in *The Atlantic*:

> *Cities are our greatest invention, not because of the scale of their infrastructure or their placement along key trade routes, but because they enable human beings to combine and recombine their talents and ideas in new ways. With their breadth of skills, dense social networks and physical spaces for interactions, great cities and metro areas push people together and increase the kinetic energy between them.*
>
> *As highly skilled people concentrate in these places, the rate of innovation accelerates, new businesses are created, and productivity – and, ultimately, pay – grows. Wages generally increase with city size, as opportunities for specialization and interaction multiply. Pay for manufacturing workers tends to rise about the national average, for instance, as communities grow beyond 120,000 people. The wages for knowledge-based jobs were markedly higher than average in locations where labor markets number one million people or more. In*

other words, the critical mass for knowledge work is higher than for manufacturing: the knowledge economy thrives at a larger scale.[60]

It would be hard to put the case more clearly or succinctly than that. In another *Atlantic* article, he notes that we are hardly done with this transformation yet:

Gradually, our great complexes of cities and suburbs are being knit into mega-regions – giant city-states that are home to millions upon millions of people and generate billions and in some cases trillions of dollars of economic activity. Driving this is not just our individual choices and preferences but the very logic of economic development. Geographic concentration and clustering speeds the transmission of new ideas, increases the underlying productivity of people and firms, and generates powerful economies of scale.[61]

According to McKinsey, just 380 cities in developed nations generated half of the world's GDP in 2007. The company predicts that the top 600 cities will generate 60 percent of global GDP growth through 2025.[62]

A modern American homily has it that "if you can't run with the big dogs, stay on the porch." So, will the 21st Century be a time when Edge cities that can't run with the big dogs in the Center have to stay on the porch and out of the running, economically speaking?

There are reasons to doubt it.

Hollow at the Center

The experience of big cities in the industrialized world since the 1970s makes clear that size and centrality do not guarantee prosperity. In North America, no place illustrates this better than one so central to an industry that it was nicknamed Motor City. The government, businesses and people of Detroit so steadfastly refused to recognize the changes transforming the automotive industry and broader economy over past decades that the city was forced into the largest municipal bankruptcy in American history in July 2013.

Fifty years ago, Detroit was rich and its automakers produced nearly every car sold in the United States. Of the 1.8 million people who lived there then, only 700,000 remain, of whom fewer than 20% have more than a secondary school diploma. Its long-term debt is estimated to be US$18.2 billion, about half of which consists of unfunded retirement benefits and the other half the result of spending $100 million more each year than it received in taxes. [63]

Detroit is hardly the only city at the Center to be hollowed out by economic change to which it failed to respond. New York, the self-styled "greatest city on earth," nearly defaulted on its debts in 1975. It was once said of Manchester, the UK's second city, that "what Manchester does today, the rest of the world does tomorrow." That was before the city lost 150,000 jobs to deindustrialization from 1960 to 1980.[64]

In Germany, the cities of Dortmund and Essen are the center of the Ruhr industrial region, which was the keystone of Germany's economic recovery from the Second World War. In the 1970s, they were among hardest hit by the decline of the coal and steel industries and took decades to diversify their economies and return to health.[65] Bangkok, Jakarta and Seoul were devastated by the 1997 Asian financial crisis, when a mighty real estate bubble collapsed. Their recovery required only years rather than decades, however, because it took place during the legendary period of emerging market growth that preceded 2010.[66]

It is good to be the king, to be a city at the Center, but Shakespeare also noted that the wearing of a crown makes the head beneath it uneasy.

Big, central cities are hard to run because of their sheer size, not to mention the multiplicity of groups and factions with entrenched interests to defend against every proposed change. Their size gives them massive momentum, so that in good times, growth in their economies, populations and political clout can seem unstoppable. Equally, it can take decades for bad decisions and willful blindness to lead to catastrophe. Once a downward spiral begins, however, it can achieve a momentum every bit as powerful.

According to research by Robert Inman of the Wharton School at the University of Pennsylvania, cities are vulnerable if they have high costs and charge high business and residential taxes without delivering matching levels of service. High costs may be driven by excess staffing, high salaries for low productivity (often enforced by union contracts), bad financial management, or high social service costs driven by poverty.

Such an imbalance between taxes and services tends to drive out middle and upper-income taxpayers and businesses. Professor Inman estimated that the American city of Philadelphia – with both a large poor population and highly unionized city workforce – lost more than 200,000 jobs over 30 years solely because of increases in the city's wage tax rate, which tended to fall most heavily on employers. [67]

New Models at the Edge

Clearly, what makes the difference is not being big or being central, but knowing what to do and finding the collective political will to do it. Cities on the Edge are as capable of possessing this wisdom and determination as any city at the

Center. The scales may be tipped in favor of bigger cities by the bigger salaries they can offer to attract managerial talent and the greater resources they can throw at problems. But weighing on the other side of the scale is something that no city had to contend with fifty years ago: connectivity.

The network convergence that has so benefited Center cities – of transportation, people, money and knowledge – is increasingly being counterbalanced by the convergence of the digital network. In an age when knowledge, innovation and, increasingly, money travel in the form of internet Protocol packets, smaller, more nimble Edge cities can find themselves with an unforeseen advantage in controlling their economic destinies. The Edge just isn't as far from the Center as it used to be.

In its 2007 annual report, the United Nations Population Fund actually predicted that – despite all the attention paid to megacities – most of the developing world's urban growth would take place in much smaller ones.

The megacities are still dominant, but they have not grown to the sizes once projected. Today's megacities account for 4 percent of the world's population and 9 percent of all urban inhabitants. This is an important slice of the urban world, but it will probably not expand quickly in the foreseeable future. Many of the world's largest cities – Buenos Aires, Calcutta, Mexico City, Sao Paulo and Seoul – actually have more people moving out than in, and few are close to the size that doomsayers predicted in the 1970s.[68]

So, what does an Edge city look like when it turns to communication networks to give it a competitive advantage? It could well look like Moncton, New Brunswick, Canada.

In the 1980s, this city of 76,000 people experienced the perfect economic storm. The Canadian National railroad, which had long operated its repair facility for eastern Canada in Moncton, announced that it was closing down the Moncton Shops. Eaton's, a national department store chain, closed its distribution center and several local factories went belly up. Because rail and transportation had dominated its economy for so long, Moncton's workforce was educated for an era of manual work, not the emerging knowledge economy. The city's downtown had a high vacancy rate and plunging municipal budgets could not keep up with maintenance of city infrastructure.

"I remember the boarded-up shops," said George LeBlanc, who was first elected Mayor in 2008 after nine years on the City Council. "Anybody looking for opportunity in Moncton quickly learned to 'go down the road' to Toronto."

Moncton responded to the crisis by organizing the first of a series of regional economic development planning exercises in 1989. Government and business leaders formed and agreed to fund the Greater Moncton Economic Commission, the first regional economic development agency. They forged a partnership between local and provincial government to focus on attracting new business to the region.

In the late Eighties, the hot opportunity turned out to be call centers. Both outbound and inbound call centers experienced a boom in this period, and Moncton had the potential to benefit because of its low costs and one special attribute: it had one of the most bilingual workforces in Canada, with half of the population speaking both French and English.

The incumbent carrier NBTel (now Aliant Telecom), proved willing to step up to meet new requirements. The first Canadian carrier to build a 100% digital network in the early 1990s, Aliant created a suite of services to support call centers, including the leasing (rather than purchase) of costly switches and systems for home-based employees.

One key to its success came as the result of an unlikely decision back in the days when NBTel was a provincial monopoly. As the fiber-optic investment boom swept through the telecom industry, NBTel decided not to concentrate fiber along the highways and rail lines connecting major population centers, like most carriers. Instead, it ran fiber circuits to central offices throughout the thinly-populated province, giving places with mere hundreds of citizens a point of presence on the information highway. Inherited by Aliant, this underlying infrastructure proved to be a hidden asset of tremendous value for Moncton.

Through energetic lobbying, Moncton won the support of New Brunswick's government to actively promote the city as a place to base telecom-intensive service and IT operations. The province helped the city to attract call centers for over two dozen national and international firms including ExxonMobil, UPS, FedEx and the Royal Bank of Canada. By 1994, call centers had become a major source of new jobs, exceeding goals set in 1991. But the 1994 plan recognized that success in call center development was not enough; the next step was to focus on knowledge businesses – natural and applied sciences, business and finance, computer programming and information systems.

More partnerships ensued. Moncton tapped the resources of national and provincial government agencies to spur attraction and start-up of knowledge-based businesses. The Greater Moncton Strategic Partnership linked local government with universities, colleges, local media and leading-edge companies to fund talent-attraction marketing in order to feed the rising demand for qualified people.

In 2008, the call center sector paid more than C$290 million in payroll and generated a total of C$765 million in regional economic activity. But Moncton increasingly focused on helping homegrown IT-intensive businesses prosper, from the Atlantic Lottery Corporation and Red Ball internet to PropertyGuys.com, which is now North America's largest private home sales network. The community's hospitals have since become catalysts for an emerging life sciences cluster focusing on medical informatics, biomarkers and biostatistics. The Atlantic Cancer Research Institute is the largest in Atlantic Canada. L'Université de Moncton is well known for research on cellular lipid metabolism and is home to New Brunswick's only medical school, while private company DDx Health Strategies is pioneering in remote support for the pharmaceutical industry and MedSenses offers health care e-learning solutions.

A local entrepreneur went from working as a video game repair technician to creating a state-of-the-art video lottery machine system. Global lottery giant GTECH acquired this Moncton-grown company in 2004 and was itself acquired in 2006 by Italy's Lottomatica, which chose to maintain production of the systems in Moncton. The result has been a gaming cluster, which now includes a unit of Oracle and a significant number of homegrown companies and development centers for multinationals.

By 2006, almost 45 out of every 1,000 workers in the Moncton Census Metropolitan Area (CMA) worked in customer service, information or related clerk positions, compared with an average of 12 for Canada. Moncton had witnessed a 300% increase in employment in ICT companies, a 153% increase in employment for graphic designers and illustrators, and a 43% increase in jobs for writers and translators. While New Brunswick suffered a net loss of 3,900 people from 2001 to 2006, the Greater Moncton area gained 6,800.

Moncton ploughed economic growth back into infrastructure, building a new City Hall, widening bridges and roads and opening up parcels of land to development of corporate headquarters, call centers and media studios. One of the most satisfying milestones was the opening of the Emmerson Business & Technology Park on the brownfield site that had been home to CN's Moncton Shops. The developer, Canada Lands Company, put C$50 million into cleanup and redevelopment of the 249-acre site, which also includes the CN Sportplex and residential units.

In from the Edge of Europe

When Estonia emerged from fifty years of Soviet rule in 1991, the new nation did a very strange thing. It got really excited about a suggestion by then-Ambassador to the US and now President Toomas Hendrik Ilves to bring PCs with internet connections into every school by 1999. It was strange because Estonia could barely pay its teachers and its schools were as physically ruined as most of its Soviet-era infrastructure. Computers in schools were not an obvious answer – but they came to stand for a bottomless thirst to emerge from the shadow of the Soviet Union and enter a very different world.

Estonia opened its telecom, banking and other industries to foreign investment, drastically liberalized regulations, and convinced NGOs like the Soros Foundation and the UN Development Program to create internet access points across the nation. The government funded one of the most advanced e-government platforms in Europe, giving citizens access to a vast range of services from regulatory filings to healthcare, tax payments to legally binding digital signatures. It has since decided to fund a nationwide fiber network called Estwin, which aims to connect every residence, business and government facility with speeds up to 100 Mbps by 2015.

Tallinn, Estonia's capital and home to 400,000 people, rapidly became the hub of ICT education, expertise and industry, home to the Tallinn University of Technology and Tallinn Business Park. But Tallinn's future, like that of Estonia, looks to the west. Estonia became a member of the European Union in 2004 and joined the euro in 2011, just in time for the worst of the economic crisis. And slowly, with great determination, the city is using its digital infrastructure to move from the Edge closer to the Center of Europe.

NATO opened its Cooperative Cyber Defense Centre of Excellence in Tallinn in 2008 to take advantage of the network resources and deep technology expertise to be found there. Tallinn's IT community earned its stripes in cyber-security in 2007 when Estonian government and business became the target of a massive series of cyber-attacks, which were intently studied by governments and militaries around the globe. Though the evidence is murky, it appeared to point to Russian officials upset over plans by Estonia to relocate Soviet-era grave markers.

Tallinn's IT companies, which got their start with Estonian government contracts, are rapidly expanding outward. Located in Europe's northeast corner, they must struggle for international recognition and the kind of cross-border business connections that generate stronger growth. Tallinn's government has made it a priority to support the internationalization of its technology sector, from setting up a tech demo center for overseas visitors to encouraging the birth of Garage48. This series of business "pitch" events got its start in Tallinn and has since gone international.

One of the earliest success stories was Skype, founded in Estonia but headquartered in Luxembourg and now a division of Microsoft. Other Tallinn ICT companies going global now include ZeroTurnaround, which is transforming how programmers around the world develop, test and run Java applications, and Fits.Me, which offers a virtual fitting room for online clothing sales, using digital mannequins capable of mimicking almost 100,000 different body shapes.

On the Edge of the Capital

Taoyuan Metropolis, with its 2.2 million people, might not ordinarily be considered on the Edge. But like Oakland, California (outside San Francisco) or Offenbach, Germany (outside Frankfurt), it is a big place on the Edge of a much bigger one. To the north, Taoyuan borders the Taipei metropolitan area, home to 6.9 million people as well as Taiwan's national government. Its southern and western regions, however, are rural, mountainous and sparsely populated.

Tying together these very different regions is the goal of an aggressive public and private investment program. The city is investing US$100m in a conduit network for optical fiber that connects 13 cities and towns as well as remote villages in the mountains. By laying all that conduit, the city is drastically reducing the broadband deployment costs for private carriers, and they are responding by rapidly building out a fiber backbone linking WiMAX 4G towers. Global Mobile Corp., a competitive carrier, has installed base stations and achieved a 75% residential penetration rate in its service area. Chunghwa Telecom, the former monopoly provider, is collaborating with city government to install Wi-Fi hotspots in the city's convenience stores as well as public facilities. The convenience store network has unusual importance in Taiwan. The nation boasts the world's highest density of such stores, and residents turn to them, not just for newspapers, rice rolls and cigarettes, but for banking, postal services, tax filing, transit tickets and many other private and public services. [69]

But when it comes to shifting Taoyuan from the Edge to the Center, nothing beats the impact of something called the Aerotropolis project.

On the 4th of July in 2008, the first direct flight from China in sixty years landed at the Taiwan Taoyuan International Airport.[70] From that symbolic wheels-down moment, air traffic and economic activity have grown swiftly. From a zero base in 2007, direct Taiwan-China passenger traffic totaled 9 million annual seats in 2011, according to airline research company OAG. [71]

Under President Ma Ying-Jeou, former mayor of Taipei, the national government has identified 12 "i-Taiwan" public construction projects with a total budget of nearly US$133bn through 2016. One is the Taoyuan Aerotropolis, in which the government plans to invest $40bn and attract matching investment from the private sector, leading to the creation of 80,000 new jobs and $20bn in additional economic activity by 2021.

An aerotropolis is an urban model that identifies airports as central locations around which to grow a city by facilitating the flow of people, goods, capital, information and technology to the global marketplace. The national government will retain control over the airport and a successful free trade zone (FTZ) at the center, while surrounding development will be the responsibility of the city and private industry.

The FTZ, managed by Farglory, is the only one among 700 worldwide to combine an air cargo terminal, freight forwarders' warehouse, logistics center and value-added industrial park. The facilities are connected by automated cargo handling and tracking systems. A new transit system will speed connections from the airport and free trade zone to most of northern Taiwan including the capital.[72]

The first rule of such massive projects is that they take far longer and cost enormously more than anyone projects. The plan calls for acquiring more than 6,000 hectares (23,000 square miles) of land from its owners, and the complexity of the negotiations is hard to imagine, let alone manage.

But you may not want to bet against them. Taiwan ranks first in the world at what the World Economic Forum *Global Competitiveness Report* calls "state of cluster development." At the end of 2012, the national government was operating 62 industrial parks housing 13,600 companies.

Taoyuan is no slouch at industrial development, either. At the end of 2011, the city already had more than 10,000 factories, many of them owned by Taiwan's top 500 manufacturing companies. The logistics industry is already centered there, including warehouses for UPS, FedEx, TACT, Farglory, Everterminal and EGAC, moving cargo worth almost US$17bn per year. In the 11 months from October 2011 to August 2012, the city gained commitments for US$1.5bn in new factory investment.

Moving Mountains

It's nice to have one's central government provide a tsunami of public investment that gets the industrial development and real estate communities slathering at the mouth. But most cities at the Edge can only dream of such bounty. For them, the question is how to leverage their slender resources to seize the opportunities created by network connectivity.

The first step is to make sure that the required connectivity is in place. Not every city or region needs 100 Mbps or 1 Gbps running into every office, factory and home, any more than they need a superhighway connecting every home and business. "Gig Cities" are a hot topic right now, as they rightly should be: a lucky few places are deploying broadband capacity so extreme that we don't even know what to do with it yet, and the excitement of the story lies in finding out.

But in practical terms, what Intelligent Communities need is "good enough now" – widespread availability and penetration of broadband at speeds in the 5-20 Mbps range at affordable prices. For many Edge cities, particularly in rural areas, that fundamental level of service is still out of reach, but the gaps are narrowing every year.

Infrastructure, however, is just opportunity. There it lies in the ground or up on towers in the air, waiting for somebody to turn it into value. Doing *that* requires something that is frequently in short supply in Edge cities. Faith.

It is said that faith is a commitment to live as if certain things were true and thereby to help make them so. Once Edge cities – their leaders and their people – start to believe that the Edge is a great place to be, possibilities open.

Moncton's resurgence began when city leaders decided that there was no reason their community should not be the ideal location for global companies like ExxonMobil, UPS and FedEx – and then went in search of help in reeling them in from business, local educators and provincial government. When it began to achieve success with call centers, leaders raised their sights to the higher goal of creating or attracting a cluster of businesses whose success depended on information technology and access to connectivity. It went on to build the first free outdoor wireless mesh network in Canada to support local business and bring the internet to city buses.

Tallinn's story is no different. At the time of independence in 1991, it was a basket case. Things got worse in 1999, when Russia was hit with a debt crisis and Estonia's export markets, still dominated by old ties, nearly collapsed. Yet, only six years passed before Estonia was in the EU.

And to understand the faith that is driving Taoyuan, one need only compare it with another city that rests on the Edge of a real Center. The city of Newark is the largest by population in the state of New Jersey. Located across the harbor from New York City, it is home to Port Newark, a major container terminal, and Newark Liberty International Airport, one of the busiest in the United States. But until 2006, when a six-term mayor declined to run again after being indicted on 33 counts of fraud, the city was a byword for corruption, poverty, crime and urban decay. *Time* magazine called it America's most dangerous city in 1996. Newark's airport, seaport and major logistics and financial businesses might as well have been operating under a dome for all of the prosperity they brought to the rest of the city.

It took the election of Mayor Corey Booker, who went on to a successful run for the US Senate, to generate hope. With the help of state government, the city has attracted $1bn in development projects as well as major philanthropic investments in its school system. The story of its recovery is still in the beginning stages – but it is not a story that the Edge city of Taoyuan needs to tell, because its leaders never lost their faith in a better future. By 2016, Taoyuan Metropolis will no longer be on any identifiable Edge – it will occupy the Center of a regional transport network that sets value flowing inward from throughout the Asia-Pacific.

Faith may seem an odd note on which to end a discussion of economic development in the digital age. But faith, put into action, is a consistent trait of Intelligent Communities. The continued explosive growth of broadband connectivity has the potential to close much of the gap separating the Edge from the Center – to lower the mountains and raise the valleys, in economic terms – but potential becomes reality only when cities at the Edge develop faith in a different future and in their own capacity to seize it.

CHAPTER SEVEN

The Light from Dying Stars

One of the best things about living in a place which actually is dark at night – a place on the edge or even further, such as a farm or small village – is that you can look to the sky on a clear night and see magnificent clusters of stars. The universe unfolds its promise and mystery to envelop you. There are 6,000 stars visible to the naked eye in places where light pollution or bright lights do not hinder the view. While some stars stand alone, others are clustered in celestial neighborhoods. They appear bright, alive and eternal – but it is an illusion. Science has taught us that we are looking at the past when we have stars in our eyes. Even our own Sun's light arrives on Earth eight minutes after it is created. Because the universe is so vast, light from distant stars takes much, much longer to reach us, which means that the light we see tonight may come from a star that burned up its fuel and went out a hundred years ago. We will not notice until the last of its light reaches our eyes.

The same can be true of communities – and there are many of them – in the late stages of decline. In these places, you sense that something is not as it was and not quite right, despite the familiar motions of daily life. They are carrying on, but not moving forward. In these places, a phrase from a Pink Floyd song (by way of Ralph Waldo Emerson), comes to mind: we see people "hanging on in quiet desperation." It was of these places that Senator Barack Obama spoke during his 2008 Presidential campaign, when he said:

You go into these small towns and the jobs have been gone now for 25 years and nothing has replaced them. These places fell through each successive administration, which said that, somehow, they would regenerate. But they have not. And it is not surprising that they get bitter; they cling to guns or religion or antipathy toward people who aren't like them or anti-immigrant sentiment or anti-trade sentiment as a way to explain their frustrations.

The Senator caught a lot of flak from his opponents for his supposed disrespect for people who own guns or go to church, but the honesty of his comment has outlasted the critics. In such places, there is a palpable desperation that bites all the way into the soul of a place. Or sometimes, its opposite: the anger and defiance that is the product of fear, as people seek to defend themselves from an enemy they can never quite come to grips with. People remain friendly and helpful, but there is a shadow over the place and young people confess that "they cannot wait to get out." Woody Allen once wrote that "My one regret in life is that I am not someone else." That is the sentiment of a dying town.

In small villages and towns, the most measurable sign of decline is revealed through the numbers of young people who have left, or continue to migrate out, many never to return. The 2010 US Census showed that only 16% of Americans live in rural areas, down from 72% a century ago, and projected on current trends that many of these areas would shrink to virtually nothing by 2050. Areas like the Great Plains, Appalachia, Texas and parts of the South are likely to face the steepest population declines, as young adults leave and the people remaining grow older.[73]

In India, the urban population doubled to 31% of the total from 1951 to 2011. Large numbers of young people are migrating to the overcrowded cities because their rural birthplaces offer too few employment opportunities.[74] In China in 2009, there were 145 million rural migrants living in urban areas, equal to about 11% of the total population.[75]

The dying star effect is visible in every corner of the world, caused by migration from rural areas to cities, from declining to growing cities, and from countries offering less opportunity to those offering more. In 2014, the sixth largest French city, according to French writer Pascal Bruckner, was not in France at all, but across the Channel in London. France has witnessed a massive migration out of the country since 2004, as nearly two million French citizens have chosen to leave. According to Bruckner the French nation has not found its footing in the entrepreneurially charged decades of the digital era. A 2005 survey revealed that nearly 75% of French youth aspired to become, not owners of their own business, as a vast majority of youth in Stockholm did in 2009, but rather government workers. To them, a future without risk seems preferable to a future of possibility.[76]

If Bruckner is right, a massive number of France's best and most industrious have decided to take their chances in innovation-driven economies in Australia, Brazil, Canada, the USA and China. The last exodus of this type, Bruckner notes, occurred 100 years ago, when nearly the same number of people fled France because of the revocation of the Edict of Nantes. "However, today's migration," Bruckner wrote in City Journal, "isn't politically or religiously motivated. It is economic." If these statistics hold, the risk-takers and knowledge workers of French society are on their way out. They are young. Nearly 70% have not yet celebrated their 40th birthday and most all hold advanced degrees.[77]

The French private sector shed 360,000 jobs in the second quarter of 2013, placing even more pressure on those left behind. Bruckner notes that the wounds caused by this economic inertia have left a social and psychological scar on those left behind. "A nation that not long ago brandished its language as the natural idiom of the human race now seems to know how to groan, rehearse the past, lick its wounds, and endlessly enumerate its failings, though with a suspicious self-satisfaction." The great cultural genius of France seems unable to grasp any clear vision of the future. Its intellectual production includes dozens of books affecting, as Bruckner calls it, "the charm of despair."[78]

Yet a few places refuse to let their light go out. They include the exceptional city of Issy-les-Moulineaux, a successful community on the outskirts of Paris, where Microsoft located its largest campus outside of the US. Led for more than two decades by Mayor Andre Santini, Issy has become an important technology hub and start-up haven bordering Paris. The story of its success began in the 1990s, when Mayor Santini re-envisioned this dilapidated industrial zone as a center for high technology. Issy was the first city in France to offer businesses a choice of communications carriers, was one of the first to deploy free Wi-Fi and has one of the highest broadband penetration rates in the nation. It invests continuously in making ICT an essential part of life for citizens and organizations, from "cyber-kindergartens" and computer training to online government and digital arts. With an employment rate close to 95% of the working age population, Issy has the distinction of having 15% more jobs than residents, and a web-savvy population in which 98% of respondents told a recent survey that the internet had fundamentally changed their lives.

The Fearless Community

In cities flaming-out of once stellar neighborhoods, it is nostalgia rather than a vision for the future which becomes central to the daily storytelling of the place. And as any athlete going through a bad patch can tell you, when self-esteem plunges, performance follows. It plunges so much in some places that parents actually encourage their children to leave, and when those young people are asked by friends or employers where they come from, they answer, "You wouldn't know it. It is in the middle of nowhere."

Not for adventure or to taste the delightful possibilities of the world do they leave, but for economic need and a thirst for something better: a true and deeper meaning of place, which includes a good job, an opportunity to participate in the energy of thriving culture, or just to have coffee in a café where there is both Wi-Fi and the opportunity for an interesting discussion. The place of their birth and their heritage has not only become bare of any economic or social essentials, it has become so apparently toxic that no social antibiotic can cure it.

For those left behind, denial often sets in. Denial is a powerful coping mechanism for communities that simply do not believe what is happening to them "We can handle it," is the phrase you hear. "We will come back. It is a cycle and it will come back around." But so long as they are in denial, no change is possible. A lucky few go into spontaneous remission – the current rise of fracking is causing boom times in many rural parts of the United States – but resource-driven economies suffer from massive booms and busts, with the boom times benefiting a privileged few most of all.

Among the world's most competitive economies, there are very few at or near the top that arrived there because they found oil, developed fracking or mined coal. The winners tend to be like Singapore, which has no natural resources beyond its people but under the slogan "Thinking nation, Learning Nation" has managed to build a first-world economy that is the envy of its region

As Thomas L. Friedman pointed out in a 2012 *New York Times* column, the best way to keep from being left behind is to develop a new ecosystem. The best of places, he wrote, "will be cities and towns that combine a university, an educated populace, a dynamic business community and the fastest broadband connections on earth. These will be the job factories of the future." What he didn't say is how much fearlessness is required. [79]

Not all communities are this fearless. Not even the new giants of the global economy, like China and India, who continue to see a steady brain drain of their top students and graduates. Canada welcomed a record 100,000 students in the same year, 26% of them from China.[80] Of the 820,000 students who came to the US to study in the 2012-13 school year, 29% were from China, with lesser percentages from India, South Korea and Saudi Arabia.[81] The US issues H-1B temporary visas to foreign workers, largely in technology fields; the two top countries receiving such visas in 2012 were India (64% of the total) and China (8% of the total).[82]

While many places seem helpless to stop this outward flood, Intelligent Communities tend to focus sharply on this issue. In Shinsha Elementary school in the agricultural district of Taichung, Wu Rong-feng, the head of education for the city took one of this book's writers around to demonstrate the degree to which digital opportunities prevail.

"We believe libraries and schools to be the center of the community," he said. "We concentrate digital opportunities here." These include Digital Opportunity Centers and mobile tablets given to students. The Digital Opportunity Centers

(DOCs) are tied to economic development programs, like one that helps farmers find value-added in their products. There is a decidedly mercantile mindset, rather than strictly social welfare, driving these programs.

The incumbent carrier, Chunghwa, has also done something that in many places incumbents need to be strong-armed into doing: providing competitive last mile access for citizens. Mike Lin, a social entrepreneur, worked with Microsoft until the Chunghwa Foundation captured his interest. Lin has pushed Chunghwa into donating network service and stabilizing neighborhoods through a Digital Good Neighbor Project. He wants to influence government to continue to view the digital divide as an opportunity to yield, in his words, "a digital dividend" instead.

An e-book library culture has flourished as a result of these collective efforts. The e-readership rate is up to 58% of the population and continues to be driven by the city's Cultural Affairs Department. In a nation whose reading rates are high because, in the words of Lin, "we are a nation of people thirsty for learning," the programs help alleviate a concern about the next generation fleeing Taiwan.

Australia is one of the world's advanced economies, with a gross domestic product per capita of US$43,000, ranking 10th in the world in 2013.[83] But when it came to access to broadband, the nation trailed countries that it competes with not only in penetration but in average broadband speeds. The reasons were not far to seek. Nearly all of its broadband services were provided over an aging copper network that, in many places, was challenged to provide decent phone service. Nearly all of that copper network was owned by Telstra, which enjoyed a near monopoly on local, long-distance and international communications.

In 2007, Australia's government announced the launch of the National Broadband Network, a staggeringly ambitious plan to deploy a fiber-optic network, augmented by satellite service in the most remote areas, to bring high-speed, high-quality broadband to every Australian at competitive prices regardless of location. Budgeted at A$27 billion and financed by public debt, NBN began rollout of the network in 2009 and the first services went live in Tasmania in July 2010. Since, then it has been subject to the problems, delays and cost increases typical of such massive projects. According to *The Australian*, a strategic review by Australia's Parliament in 2012 found that the costs were likely to spiral to between A$40 and $70 billion depending on future design decisions. Major contractors have decided to walk away from the project, sometimes forfeiting millions of dollars in penalties, because the rollout has been slower than predicted. The discovery of asbestos in the Telstra conduits where NBN needs to run its fiber has not helped.[84]

The inquiry is being led by Stephen Conroy, a member of the opposition Labour party. He is seeking to defend his legacy against a Conservative Government than is viscerally opposed: it was Conroy, as Minister of Communications in the previous government, who took NBN from an idea to a reality being deployed in 40 sites around Australia. This is the nature of big infrastructure projects, and like most of them, this one is likely to proceed and deliver benefits immeasurably greater than its investment. Subscriber revenues are expected be between A$10 and $18 billion by 2024, providing a means to pay down the debt, whatever it turns out to be. The truly interesting thing about the discussion is the fact that the Australian government will spend A$1.2 trillion on public healthcare and A$200 billion on defense over the same 10-

year period that deployment should require, which makes the NBN seem like a bargain.

For a small city like Prospect, a suburb of Adelaide, the NBN is key to the future. Prospect is a prosperous place already, with a high percentage of skilled workers bringing home above-average disposable income. But the headline numbers hide concerns typical of Australian suburbs. As a "bedroom community," it sends most of its skilled workers to Adelaide to earn their living, which stunts its own potential for growth. Its telecom infrastructure consists of copper wire so aged that one technician told Council that "residents are lucky to be getting telephone calls, let alone use broadband."

Prospect's activist Council successfully lobbied national government to make the city a Stage Two deployment site for the NBN. Network construction began in August 2012 with completion targeted for 2014. In the meantime, Council separately chose to fund a fiber network to connect all government sites and has persuaded private sector carriers to in-fill their wireless networks to eliminate holes in coverage.

While it waited impatiently for network activation, Prospect invested grant funding in projects to create a local digital economy. The city is now delivering digital training to hundreds of individuals and local businesses. Much of this takes place at the Digital Hub, an NBN demonstration facility completed in 2013 that showcases home and business technologies made possible by high-quality broadband. Another grant has gone into developing e-government applications including videoconferencing of Council sessions and a mobile-ready web portal for citizen interactions with local government. More than half of Prospect's small businesses are home-based, and the city has launched a two-year training program in digital entrepreneurship. One focus of that program has been on Prospect's thriving arts community, which has thronged training sessions. Prospect is also driving technology into its support for the arts with a digital Artist in Residence program and Club 5082, where young musicians get a chance to perform live and take away their performances in digital form to help promote their music. When the NBN is finally ready for Prospect, the city will be more than ready for its broadband future.

Distribution Point for Pathology

One of our authors comes from a small town in northern New York State, and has seen the dying light with his own eyes. It was once the proud seat of a county and a critical hub for the railroad network and Erie Canal system. It produced the legendary Hicock Belt, an endearing symbol of baseball excellence to America's baseball fans, as well as peppermint, which the local Hotchkiss Company exported around the world along with other essential oils. Neighborhoods populated by Italian and Dutch immigrants were stable and tidy, their residents working steady jobs for the railroad, agricultural factories and manufacturers. Most owned their own homes and took the pride of owners in their community.

But if the transportation infrastructure of the canal and railroad made the town, a competing infrastructure was its undoing. The construction of the New York State Thruway bypassed the town, trains soon followed suit, and so commenced the long decline of Lyons, set among the peaceful rolling drumlins of the Finger Lakes region.

As the young, the entrepreneurial and the highly educated moved away, the character of the town changed. It devolved into a distribution point for social pathologies. County and state welfare services and a greatly expanded police force now deal with a range of serious problems. An entrenched and increasingly prominent drug culture has emerged. A generation of chronically unemployed or underemployed African-American, Puerto Rican and poor white citizens, many of them transient, now rent their homes and struggle. Its two schools are in shambles and it is difficult to name an employer of any substance. Most businesses downtown are gone, with a Wal-Mart situated four miles outside of town. Where there were formerly two hospitals, the nearest emergency room is now nearly 10 miles away. Where there were three major hotels in the heart of the village, the two ramshackle motels on the edge of town today could serve as the set of a movie about drifters in America.

A family-owned movie theatre closed but was re-opened a few years ago thanks to the generosity of a former family member. He does not live there, however, but in North Carolina, where he started a successful home building business which scaled mightily and employed other former residents of the village, who also moved there.

If this sounds like a eulogy for a small town in Upstate New York, it is not meant to be. It is an extended snapshot of a place in rural America which may or may not be a dying star. There are signs of life. By 2014, the region, known as the Finger Lakes, was undergoing a slow revival. The State of New York, working cooperatively with educators and the local municipalities, established one of the first "technology farms" in the area. Located in Geneva, New York, the Cornell Agriculture and Food Technology Park was identified during its formation in 2007 by the Intelligent Community Forum as an example of how a place that had been left behind could find its footing again.

The Park is an incubator located in a 72-acre apple orchard in Geneva, New York. It is a nonprofit joint venture among Cornell University, the city of Geneva and the State of New York, which aims to create, retain and expand technology-based businesses focusing on agriculture and foodstuffs. Opening with 3 tenants and one lab in 2005, it is now home to 10 emerging businesses operating in two labs and four production facilities. The Farm prides itself on the success of Cheribundi, originally called Cherrypharm, which uses one fruit, tart cherries, to produce eleven products. The company's success has led to expansion and, this year, it entered the competitive tea and fruit drinks market. Other companies include a food oils startup that uses pumpkin seeds as raw material, which grow in abundance in the Finger Lakes.

The Technology Farm alone will not change the fact that, in the larger county, one out of every three people below the age of 18 lives below the US poverty line. But it is a start. The reverberations from a burst in the innovation surrounding wine-growing, foods and research may have a broader impact on employment

Believing What You See

When we look at the night sky, we should not necessarily believe what see, because we may be looking at old news from the far side of the galaxy. The stagnation and decline of places are not always what they seem, either. In the 2014 annual letter of the Gates Foundation, Bill Gates wrote about the myth of the developing world that never improves and of the poor countries that are doomed to stay poor. Mr. Gates put it this way:

> *The global picture of poverty has been completely redrawn in my lifetime. Per-person incomes in Turkey and Chile are where the United States level was in 1960. Malaysia is nearly there, as is Gabon. And that no-man's-land between rich and poor countries has been filled in by China, India, Brazil, and others. Since 1960, China's*

real income per person has gone up eightfold. India's has quadrupled, Brazil's has almost quintupled, and the small country of Botswana, with shrewd management of its mineral resources, has seen a thirty-fold increase. There is a class of nations in the middle that barely existed 50 years ago, and it includes more than half of the world's population.[85]

This is happening for many reasons, but among them is certainly communications, which boosts all forms of economic, educational and social activity, and lets people everywhere learn what is possible anywhere. In *The Great Escape*, Angus Deaton wrote that "the share of people living on less than US$1 per day (in inflation-adjusted terms) has fallen nearly 15 percent, from 42 percent in 1980." He adds that while "inequality has surged" in many places, global inequality has "very likely fallen, thanks largely to the rise of Asia. Things are getting better," he adds, "and hugely so."[86]

Today's Broadband Economy allows those left behind in the current economy to seize their destinies far more quickly, cheaply and effectively than ever before. The rise of Asia, and cities such as Taichung in Taiwan, are not simply extreme versions of uncommon success. They are models: models of an approach that values collective community, that invests in infrastructure and education, and that understands an idea first suggested 2,500 years ago by the Buddha. Nothing is permanent. The fearlessness and compulsion to adapt has taken root in those places where the light from distance stars seemed to have gone out and grown cold. The speed of fiber and the endless resource of the mind are bringing forward a new universe.

Brain Gain

CHAPTER EIGHT

How 'Ya Gonna Keep 'Em Down On the Farm?

As the First World War neared its end in 1918, three New York City songwriters published a tune that turned into a smash hit. Written by Joe Young and Sam M. Lewis to music by Walter Donaldson, it was performed by the big artists of the day for many years. The chorus went:

> *How 'ya gonna keep 'em, down on the farm,*
> *After they've seen Pa-ree?*
> *How 'ya gonna keep 'em away from Broad-way;*
> *Jazzin' a-'round',*
> *And paintin' the town?*
> *How 'ya gonna keep 'em away from harm?*
> *That's a mystery;*
> *They'll never want to see a rake or plow,*
> *And who the deuce can parleyvous a cow?*
> *How 'ya gonna keep 'em down on the farm,*
> *After they've seen Paree?*

It was an amusing little ditty. But like most humor, it was funny precisely because it touched a sore spot. In 1900, farming was America's biggest job category, employing 40% of the workforce. By the end of the century, only 2% of American workers made a living there. [87]

No one, apparently, found a way to keep 'em down on the farm for long.

Why did the rural workforce decline so much? In 1920, 36 million people, or 34% of the US population, still lived in rural counties. And their numbers did not diminish: by 2004, this rural population had grown to 50 million. But the urban population grew much faster, to 253 million. As a result, that 34% of the population down on the farm in 1920 shrank to 17% of the total eight decades later.[88]

Such an enormous change had two big causes, each the product of technology. The first was a wave of mechanization that swept over agriculture and resource extraction, from gasoline-driven tractors and self-powered combines to electrical conveyors and mine ventilators. These boosted production enormously while simultaneously reducing the demand for labor and the economic prospects of rural laborers.

Fortunately, the same clanking, roaring, clattering wave was also bringing into being the modern factory, where demand for industrial labor drew people from the countryside in search of a higher standard of living. Farming, fishing, mining and oil drilling have a romantic aspect to those who have never done them, but they are hard and unforgiving labor offering volatile returns. Compared with wresting a living from the land, salaried days in a factory – even the dark and dangerous mills of the early 20th Century – proved irresistibly attractive.

The same story played out in every industrialized nation through 2000 and accelerated in the emerging market nations in the new millennium. Halfway through the 20th Century, according to the United Nations, 71% of the world's population lived in rural areas. Just sixty years later, in 2010, the percentage shrank to 49%, when a slim majority of the global population became urbanites. And that average number masks big differences. The more-developed regions led the way: their rural population fell from 47% to only 25%. But even in less-developed regions, with their much greater demand on agriculture to generate income, the rural population shrank from 82% to 55% of the whole. [89]

Natural Decrease

According to Kenneth Johnson, senior demographer at the Carsey Institute of the University of New Hampshire, 36% of counties in the United States spent the first decade of the 21st Century "in a vicious and intractable cycle of population decline that demographers call 'natural decrease' – when more people die than are born." This compares to 29% of counties in the 1990s – and that was the decade following the "farm crisis" of the Eighties, when low crop prices and declining farm incomes led to bankruptcies, family breakups and increased rates of farmer suicides. [90]

Rural America is not alone in wrestling with natural decline. Nigeria's rural population made up 84% of the total in 1960, but 50% in 2010. Mexico's rural population shrank from 49% of the population in 1960 to 22% by 2010.[91] In China, the urbanization that took almost a century in the West has happened in the past few decades. In 1979, Shenzhen was a fishing village with 20,000 people. In 2009, it had a population of 9 million and $13,600 in per-capita income, just a bit less than Taiwan or South Korea.[92] Shenzen was not an isolated example. In 1979, 81% of Chinese lived in rural areas; by 2012, more than half of China's population was urban. [93]

Natural decrease in rural areas is the endgame of our stunning success in making agriculture and resource extraction more productive. From 1980 to 2002, the number of hog farmers in Iowa dropped six times – from 65,000 in 1980 to 10,000 – but the number of hogs per farm grew seven times, from 200 to 1,400. [94]   Pork consumers certainly gained, but the profession of hog farming did not. Australia's coal-mining industry produced three times more coal per employee in 1997 (8,400 metric tonnes) than it did in 1980 (2,800 metric tonnes). During that 17 years, total employment shrank by 13%.[95]

Dealing with the Downside

This relative population decline in rural areas can have massive effects on the people who remain there. The lack of high-quality job opportunities, compared with urban areas, forces the brightest young adults to leave their communities in order to make a living. Once gone – involved in romantic relationships, making homes and raising families – only a few return. As the population shrinks in relative or actual terms, the tax and spending base supporting services, from schools to stores to cultural activities, slowly declines. Schools are consolidated, stores close up, cultural activities fade away – and each loss further erodes rural quality of life. Meanwhile, the increasing average age of the population, as deaths outweigh births, puts greater strain on social services, which are increasingly hard to afford.

Rural areas in developing nations face an additional strain – the absence of working age men. Villages in the rural areas of Mexico, India, the Philippines, China and other nations are full of young women, children and old people, while the men have left to find paying work far from home.

Some rural areas buck the trend. Many rural areas are not in crisis. Those located within driving distance of an urban center attract commuters and weekenders. Those with scenery, cultural or recreational attractions balance local enterprise with income from tourism. Some hold onto a local manufacturing base or exploit geography to become transport and logistics hubs. But these opportunities are distributed neither evenly nor with regard to the welfare of the people who occupy rural land. [96]

The Canadian Council on Learning reported in 2006 that students in rural Canada significantly underperform their urban peers. Secondary school dropout rates are nearly twice that of metro regions and the percentage of 25- to 54-year-olds with at least some post-secondary education is 10% below that of urban areas. [97]

The European Commission has found the same patterns in its member countries. Rural areas within reasonable commuting distance of population centers have continued to grow as people move outward in search of affordable housing and a better quality of life. The rural coasts of Spain, Portugal and southern France have benefited from the migration of retired people with relatively high incomes. But communities without these advantages have found the going much harder. The welfare of rural areas in Sweden, the Czech Republic and Hungary are all threatened by the migration of young people to the cities. In Romania, only one-third of the rural population has access to the public water supply network, while rural Italy is sparsely served with railway connections, broadband connections, postal and banking services. Rural areas in Europe also tend to be poorer, with a higher percentage of poorly educated people. In Hungarian villages, more than 40% of the population has no educational qualifications at all. [98]

In France, one of the biggest challenges facing farmers is not bad weather or agricultural policy but loneliness. According to an August 2011 article in *The New York Times*, "The lack of love in the countryside is a serious topic for a country that sees its bedrock in small farmers and their produce, which is supposed to be uniquely of the place where it is grown. According to the Agriculture Ministry, about 30 percent of male French farmers did not have a partner in 2009. Loneliness is particularly acute among male farmers between 18 and 35, especially cattle farmers, who generally spend more time working than others. About 36 percent of cattle farmers were single in 2009, according to the ministry." [99]

An English web site recounts the challenges of Tibenham, the seventh largest of 118 villages in South Norfolk, UK. Its population in 1845 was 749, and it was home to businesses including pubs, coal dealers, grocers, butchers and bakers, blacksmiths and wheelwrights, tailors and boot makers. By 1982, the population was 392, and the only village facilities still open were the Post Office Stores (what Americans would call a convenience store), a pub and a primary school with 2 teachers and 25 pupils. [100]

"The race is not always to the swift nor battle to the strong," wrote American journalist Damon Runyon, "but that's the way to bet." Left unchanged, these patterns of natural decrease will lead to a future very different from the past – and from the hopes and dreams of young people growing up there.

The more successful places will continue to attract money from nearby city dwellers or provide the transport and manufacturing that keep them supplied. But for the rest, it is easy to imagine a bleak future: rural lands gradually transformed into automated factories where intelligent machines produce food and extract resources; production facilities surrounded by wilderness, served by rail and road but as sparsely populated by living, breathing humans as a silicon chip fab or robotic automotive assembly line.

It sounds impossible. But anyone who worked in the textile mills that once dominated the economy of the American South can imagine the possibility all too easily. There is a bitter joke told about the textile operations that still remain there, after the flight of production to cheaper locales. The joke explains that a modern textile plant can be run just by a man and a dog. The dog's job is to keep intruders away from the fancy machinery. The man's job? To feed the dog.

Already, according to journalist Christopher Leonard in his book *The Meat Racket*, there are signs that the factory model is seizing hold in American rural areas. His book concerns Tyson Foods, the largest meat packer in America, which slaughters 135,000 head of cattle, 391,000 hogs and 41 million chickens in an average week. It also exercises enormous control over the raising of all these animals. According to Leonard, in 68% of the counties where Tyson operates, per capita income has grown more slowly over the last four decades than the average for that state, as farmers are effectively transformed into wage workers performing commodity labor.[101]

Americans who eat, rather than Americans who raise food, are the beneficiaries. In 1930, a whole dressed chicken retailed for the equivalent of $6.48 per pound in today's US dollars. Today, because of enormous gains in efficiency, the average price of chicken is $1.57 per pound.[102]

We are granted, not the future we would like, but the future we can afford. If 67% of human beings do indeed live in cities by 2030 – and another significant chunk of them occupy the surrounding suburbs and exurbs – the economic pressure to supply them from the land will be immense. That will demand higher and higher levels of productivity – getting more from the resources for less input of labor. If nothing changes, what other outcome is possible but an acceleration of the trends of the last century and a speeding up of the all-too-natural decline?

The author of the Tibenham UK web site proposes that rural residents resist this future by favoring local retailers, even if they charge higher prices, and joining local clubs and attending local churches, which are as affected by population decline as any other institution. Kind-hearted suggestions – but if the future of rural areas depends solely on good will and charitable intentions, they are doomed.

The New Urbanism

Maybe it doesn't matter. In the industrialized world, we no longer plow fields with a tree stump dragged behind a water buffalo. We no longer drive behind a team of horses or light our homes with natural gas. The iceman no longer cometh with blocks of frozen water to refrigerate our food.

Maybe the rural way of life has had its day, and it is time for us all to embrace what the city has to offer. According to the United Nations, "Wisely or not, Homo sapiens has become Homo urbanus." More than two-third of the world's population or 4.9 billion people will be urbanites by 2030. [103]

Many leading thinkers find this a cause for celebration, among them Richard Florida of the University of Toronto, who was quoted at length in a previous chapter. In acting the part of urbanization prophet, he draws on a a rich body of research that all points in the same direction. In a paper for the US Department of Housing and Urban Development, Edward Glaeser of Harvard University surveyed a century of research and found that higher population density yielded greater growth. He found that higher competition among industries – such as occurs in great cities – produced more growth. He also found that jobs in urban areas pay more. [104]

Yet another analysis finds that the top fifty largest cities on the planet contain just 7% of the world's population but already produce almost 40% of global economic activity. [105]

And apparently, we ain't seen nothing yet. If the scale of this transformation is big in the industrialized nations, according to Professor Florida, the emerging markets of the world are in for a true revolution:

> *Asia is the epicenter of the current urbanization surge. China will add at least 342 million people to its cities by 2030; India 271 million; and Indonesia, 80 million. In Latin America, which is nearing the end of the rural-urban transition, "only" 169 million people will be added. However, in Sub-Saharan Africa, 395 million people will be added to the cities over the same period, 112 percent of its current population, a larger absolute increment than China will experience.* [106]

But here's the thing. To all of his careful research and thoughtful analysis, we have a one-word response, learned from raising teenagers at the end of the 20th Century.

Duh.

Everything New is Old Again

We have known that cities are important since the founding of the world's oldest, Varansi, on the banks of the Ganges River in India 3,000 years ago. Since the time of Babylon, founded nearly two millennia ago in that fertile plain between the Tigris and Euphrates Rivers, we have known that cities are places where people, investment, ideas, arts and sciences rub against each other and by that friction produce civilization. Civilization requires first and foremost economic growth. We can only afford to think about something beyond filling our bellies when those bellies are on their way to being comfortably full. Until we have achieved a certain level of prosperity, the fruits of civilization are beyond our reach.

We are very glad that research now confirms what experience has been telling us for 3,000 years. But it is a bit like the ground-breaking 2010 study published by Cornell University professor Michael Lynn in *Archives of Sexual Behavior*. An experiment conducted by Professor Lynn was able to prove, beyond a shadow of a doubt, that waitresses with larger natural endowments, shall we say, earn bigger tips that the average restaurant server. Seriously, we are really glad that this topic is no longer up for debate. [107]

Cities work, to a greater or lesser extent, all around world. Many have benefited enormously from automation and ICT-driven trends of the past – the exploding productivity of manufacturing, the growth of the services economy and the accelerating value of knowledge and innovation. But quite a few – from the Midlands of England to Cleveland, Ohio in the US – all but crumbled under the pressure after they failed to adapt to the loss of the previous sources of their prosperity. Some of the megacities in emerging market nations may yet crumble under the unintended consequences of their growth.

Mumbai, one of emerging market's most dynamic megacities, is drowning in the by-product of its own economic success. The metropolitan region generated 11,500 metric tons of solid waste in 2011 – and had only 7,000 tons of capacity in its existing (and overflowing) landfills. Formal trash collection is almost nonexistent, leaving citizens, companies and an army of informal rag-pickers to find some way to move enough garbage aside to let the city get about its business. If Mumbai does not follow in the footsteps of its industrial world peers and establish a working waste management system, all of its furious economic growth could be for naught. [108]

Cities are old news. We can and should continue to improve how they work. We can make them smarter by installing sensors, communications links and monitor and control systems in every nook and cranny. We can demand faster, cheaper and better services for their residents and businesses. We can defend them from climate change and find ways to help them cope with population growth. These are all compelling challenges – but the innovation involved is incremental. It is all stuff that somebody knows how to do. It is the public-sector equivalent of automating a factory or creating an ATM machine to spit out cash when you need it. Management consultants have been re-engineering business processes for almost a century. Manufacturers have been sensorizing and communicating and monitoring industrial processes for decades. web software developers have been putting customer service online for years.

There is much excitement at the moment about installing those sensors, communications links and control systems into every cranny and nook of our urban centers. The European Union has a large and well-funded ICT initiative for cities. Master-planned cities, often with campuses of name-brand universities like Oxford or MIT at their heart, are rising from the desert in oil-powered Middle Eastern economies. In Asia's mega-cities, new urban oases are promising to replicate the efficiency and livability of the industrial world's best urban centers for the privileged few. They are called Smart Cities, where the traffic lights are synchronized, public servants and services are connected and Big Data analysis reveals brilliant insights about the needs and wants of citizens.

But cities are not factories, nor are they branch banking networks. The single most important thing we could do to improve the lives of people who live in the immense slums of Mumbai, for example, has nothing to do with technology. It has to do with property rights. Slum-dwellers in emerging market nations typically have only tenuous title to their property. It may have been in their family for generations but few of the poor have access to documentary proof of ownership. They may be squatting on someone else's land. They may pay a landlord for its use but there is no guarantee that the landlord has title to it, either. As a result, they are unable to realize the monetary value of that property. They cannot borrow against it to finance improvements. They cannot sell it for what it is worth – which can be quite a lot in a fast-growing city. Once people gain clear title to land, however, they begin to invest in it. They demand services from government to support their investment, which means running water, proper sanitation and reliable electricity. The pressure they can exert on their leaders grows and with it inevitably grows their standard of living.

This is just one example. The most profound challenges facing cities have little to do with technology and everything to do with people.

All of the authors of this book either lived or spent a good deal of time in New York City in the early 1980s. It was a very bad time for America's greatest metropolis. It had recently skirted bankruptcy by a whisker and a Federal loan. Its infrastructure was crumbling for lack of maintenance. The crack cocaine epidemic was spreading crime and breeding fear. Public disorder was rife, symbolized by rampant graffiti and infamous "squeegee men" who cleaned the windshields of cars stopped at traffic lights and then demanded payment.

Today, New York is one of the safest, cleanest and best-run big cities in the United States, with an economy still dominated by finance and media but featuring the fastest-growing tech sector in the country. When the biggest hurricane in decades struck in 2012, it knocked out power to parts of Manhattan and flooded much coastal development. But the transit system was largely restored within a few days and all but the worst-hit areas were back on their feet in weeks. It was a performance that would have been unimaginable in the New York City of the early Eighties.

What made the difference? Many things, as with any act of transformation. But the most important was governance. The New York City of the Eighties had been ruled by one political party for decades, and one-party rule had produced its predictable results: corruption, lack of accountability and rule by embedded interests. Then the people elected Rudolph Giuliani, a former prosecutor from the other party who owed nothing to the existing political establishment. After eight tumultuous years, Mayor Giuliani was succeeded by another leader from the wrong party who owed even less to anybody: entrepreneur and billionaire Michael Bloomberg. Between them, over 18 years, they shook up city government from top to bottom. Having founded a technology company, Mayor Bloomberg in particular made imaginative and effective use of information and communications technology. But technology was only the tool. What mattered was the determination to make things better.

Where ICT can give a push forward to better governance, it can make a substantial contribution to urban existence. But the really big challenge, the Big Hairy Audacious Goal for ICT in community life, is not in urban clusters. It is in the rural regions of our nations, whether industrial or developing. It is the unprecedented opportunity to change the dynamics that have gradually drained rural areas of so many of their people and so much of their hope.

The Middle of Nowhere is a State of Mind

Visitors to Europe are well advised to travel by train when they can. Not only is most of the continent served by an excellent railroad network, but train travel offers a chance to discover something amazing.

There is more to Europe than cities.

Duh, as our European friends might say. Of course, there is more to Europe than cities. But most tourists and business travelers go to cities and naturally develop an impression of the continent as a series of marvelous urban areas laid end to end. In truth, those cities – even ones as vast as London, Paris or Frankfurt – are insignificant islands in a mighty sea of farmland, mountain, lake and forest.

Between them are lands where, in the golden late afternoons, the shadows stand tall behind the long windbreaks of trees planted at the edge of fields, green and brown, stretching away into the distance beyond sight. People have cultivated this land for more than a thousand years, and it shows in the endless pattern of village, field and carefully groomed woodland receding to a misted horizon.

For city dwellers and their advocates, the rural lands with their farms, plains and forests represent an inconvenient distance between the places where the action is. Nothing could be further from the truth. They are the ecosystem that gives the cities life. They are the source of the air that cities breathe, the food they consume, the water they drink. In the life of nations, they offer a welcome alternative to the density and anonymity of the city. And they are places that people love. It is common for people in rural areas to be proud of their culture and arts, to care deeply about the natural beauty of the region and to treasure the ways of life that have evolved over the centuries.

For all of these reasons, it is time to stop congratulating ourselves on what is already successful and to focus on a new and exciting challenge.

In the Book of Ecclesiastes, the prophet says that there is nothing new under the sun. Damon Runyon would certainly have agreed: over the 10,000 years of human history, that has certainly been the way to bet. But in this new century, the prophet needs an update. For there *is* at long last something new under the sun. It is the global connectivity of the broadband internet.

The Broadband Economy of the 21st Century – when ICT is doing so much to eliminate distance as a barrier – offers the rural areas of the world something never seen before. The opportunity is to plug into the world at low cost regardless of location. To affordably import the world's learning and culture to enrich lives give local cultural traditions new life in a global community. To make rural areas as vital and exciting a place to grow a business or build a career as the busiest city center. All of this is possible in an economy and culture that are conducted increasingly online.

Instead of viewing rural areas as the emptiness between cities, we could come to see that they naturally have assets that urban areas struggle to reproduce: beauty, peace and a sense of belonging. They lack what urban areas come by naturally: economic vitality, intellectual stimulation and eagerness for new experiences. ICT has the potential to close that gap and make "the middle of nowhere" a meaningless concept. In our work with communities large and small, we have seen that it is not size, wealth or savvy that determines their success. Those things are results, not causes. What determines their success is their belief that they are at the burning center of the human universe. They are plugged in, switched on and pushing the outside of the envelope. They have something special to offer the world and are hungry to see what the world has to offer them. They have the power to think big even if they stay small.

We do not know how to do it yet. We do not understand how to use ICT to seize the unique opportunities and overcome the distinct challenges of rural living. When the first commercial Internet of Things browser was released in 1994, practically no one foresaw what the internet could become. We are at the same stage of this challenge: to figure out how to give the rural areas of our nations a competitive advantage using ICT that preserves their way of life into the foreseeable future. For the first time since the rural population began to lose ground in relative terms to the cities, ICT makes that possible. It is up to us to learn how it can be done.

Meeting the Rural Challenge

Ask most new residents of rural areas why they have moved there, and they will recite the same litany of benefits. Compared with urban and suburban living, there is a slower and more humane pace. There is greater respect for what has gone before, for traditional ways of thinking and living. There is less obsession with the self – with what I have compared to what you have – and more awareness of the value of community. Perhaps perception of our fellow human beings follows some kind of inverse square law. The fewer people per square mile or kilometer, the more we are likely to value each one.

There are more measurable benefits as well. Land is cheaper, regulations fewer, and public institutions are typically more eager to smooth the path of any company promising to create employment.

All of this is valuable. It helps account for why successful rural areas are successful. But it has not been enough to overcome the economic disadvantages that come with the rural lifestyle.

The biggest difference between city and country is population density. A person starting any kind of undertaking in a city can hardly avoid running into like-minded people, absorbing new ideas and being challenged by peer pressure. A wide variety of vendors, potential partners and possible employers are within arm's reach. As Derek Thompson and Jordan Weissman put it in the August 2012 issue of *The Atlantic*, "Our wealth, after all, is determined not only by our skills and talents, but by our ability to access the ideas of those around us; there's a lot to be gained by increasing the odds that smart people might bump into each other." [109]

But in the country, distances are greater between people and places. The number of interactions you can have in a day, week or month is fewer, which limits the number of like-minded people you can meet, the new ideas they can transmit and the peer pressure they can exert on you to succeed. Vendors, partners and employees are fewer and farther between. And just hanging out together can require spending a lot of time in your car or truck. It takes longer and costs more to connect the essential components of organized activity in rural areas, so the economic, social and culture return on investment tends to be lower.

Closely related to density and distance is the issue of scale. Cities have more of everything than the country: talents, information, businesses, schools, hospitals, public services, communications, transit services and transport networks, arts and culture. And money. For thousands of years, cities have been places where money concentrates and can be effectively invested to make more money. Compared to cities, rural areas have some but not much. Wealthy farmers may abound in some places, but they are more likely to put their money into global funds than local businesses, because the know-how and social structure of angel investing are weak or entirely absent.

All of this adds up, in economic terminology, to a lack scale. So, it is much more challenging to grow a business, social enterprise or artistic venture from seedling to tree. Everything may be available but not in quantities that give a natural impetus to growth. In particular, risk capital – the kind that powers fast-growing businesses and is hard to come by anywhere – may be all but absent in rural settings.

Rural areas also face a Catch-22 in their efforts to increase economic sustainability. It requires that they hang on to their best and brightest young people, who have been raised and educated locally, so that their talents can benefit the community. That's a tough assignment when electronic media in every form shows us the charisma of the city: the dynamism, the energy, the opportunity and excitement of urban living. Cities are places where jobs turn into careers, where interests become passions, where fate becomes fortune. By definition, the best and brightest want more than a dead-end job. They will only remain if they can find jobs and culture and like-minded people equal to their abilities. But how is a rural community, with its charisma deficit, to foster the creation of such jobs and culture if its best and brightest have left to seek their fortunes elsewhere?

The Rural Imperative

Can ICT truly make a dent in these disadvantages? Can it overcome the structural weaknesses of rural economies, compared with urban ones, and ensure them a vibrant economic future through robust connections to the global economy? If so, it could relieve the pressures driving migration to the cities and create breathing space, in which the inherent appeal of rural living could shine through.

The facts so far are thin on the ground, but the anecdotes point to interesting possibilities.

Remember those lonely French farmers? One of them, Patrick Maignan, was divorced in 1996 and had given up all hope of finding another mate. He worked seven days a week, after all, milking his 40 cows twice a day, and he lived far from tourist routes and mobile phone coverage. But he met a 49-year-old divorced Parisian mother of two, Claire Chollet, through an online dating site reserved for farmers, called atraverschamps.com, or "acrossthefields.com," and they bought a house together in a nearby village.

According to Luc Gagnon, founder of the Internet of Things site, it is one of a few of such sites devoted to rural people. Founded in 2001, it doubled its subscriber base in 2011 to reach over 17,000. Bertrand Blond, the founder of a competing Internet of Things site, told *The New York Times* that there is now an entire economy based on the farmer's single status. [110]

Here the marketplace is using the Internet of Things to attack the challenge of density: connecting people regardless of their current location to see if the sparks of romance can be generated across the ether. The result in this case is a happier farmer more likely to stick with his chosen profession and a net gain of three new rural residents.

In the late Nineties, the telephone company in Malaysia, together with a Malaysian university and money from the Canadian government, created a pioneering internet access project in the remotest highlands of Borneo. The residents of the village of Bario there received a computer, a generator and a satellite terminal, which connected them to the Internet of Things for the first time. The impacts were striking. Teachers used the Internet of Things to show their students the world beyond the Borneo jungle. Traditional medicine gained a helping hand from remote doctors. Bario is renowned in Malaysia for the sweet fragrance and taste of the rice it grows. Through the Internet of Things, farmers learned the true value of their crop, which gave them new bargaining power with local middlemen.

Information easily available to urban residents – schooling, healthcare and markets – leaped across the sparsely populated highlands with the help of a satellite link. It was funded by government largesse rather than market forces, but it radically transformed the quality of life for the better.

On the other side of the planet, in Arlington, Virginia, USA, is a small software company called Lemur Retail. Its founder, Will Fuentes, was planning a business trip to Seattle and needed help with a common priority: identifying potential clients and arranging to meet them. He decided to work though his local chapter of a national networking group called Startup America. Within hours, he had won some introductions, secured a temporary workspace and even received restaurant recommendations. "Before I flew out there," he told *The New York Times*, "I already had five or six meetings set up with potential clients and other key contacts, as well as one potential acquirer." [111]

Startup America is one of several nonprofit groups in the US that seek to connect startup and early stage companies around the nation. Each of its regions is led by champions who communicate via Google Groups, share an online Idea Center, and assemble at an annual national conference. The brainchild of AOL co-founder Steve Case and the Ewing Marion Kauffman Foundation, Startup America has 12,000 members in 30 of the 50 states. "Supporting startups throughout the country is the only way to make sure the American economy is firing on all cylinders," says Mr. Case. What he did not say was that, thanks to Startup America's online connections, those cylinders could be firing just as powerfully in a rural city or small town as in a metro technology hub like Alexandria, across the Potomac River from Washington DC. Mr. Fuentes reported that he found two potential clients through his connections in Seattle, and is helping his contacts in the Northwest make inroads in the Washington area. [112]

Startup America has benefited from the support of an all-star cast of deep-pocketed backers like Mr. Case. In the largely rural Canadian province of Alberta, a group of young farmers formed a similar nonprofit called Green Hectares in 2008. Founded by Wendy Snyder, a long-time rancher and cattle breeder, Green Hectares seeks to foster dynamic rural economies while bringing sustainability to agriculture. It takes existing and new community-based programs promoting entrepreneurship and smarter farming and shares them over a growing online community. To keep that community growing, Green Hectares operates a mobile computer lab and brings technology, entrepreneurship and agricultural training to communities throughout the province.

One of its Board members, Lee Townsend, is a remarkable role model. The son of a beekeeper, Lee has dramatically expanded the business of his family's TPLR Honey Farms in central Alberta. He built his own Wi-Fi network reaching every corner of the farm and uses handheld devices to collect data on the condition of his hives, which feeds a beekeeping management system that maximizes their health and output. His restless spirit led him to make connections with Japanese food importers, and a trip to Japan eventually produced a deal through which he brokers honey from across Canada to Asian markets. Japanese consumers are some of the most particular in the world when it comes to the purity and quality of food, and Townsend's ability to satisfy his Japanese partners is a rich tribute to his business and technology skills.

Green Hectares as an organization, and Townsend as an entrepreneur, are both attacking the challenge of scale. Using ICT, the nonprofit is aggregating the knowledge and skills of its subscribers, expanding those skills and energizing the more entrepreneurial among them through regular structured contact. Townsend has developed the contacts and done the deals needed to draw high-quality honey supplies from a broad region and funnel them to buyers on the far side of the planet. Those are moves that would be unimaginable without the inexpensive connecting power of information and communications technology.

Local Government at Work
Much more is possible when local rural governments step up with a strong vision of a more robust and diversified future. Castelo de Vide is an inland Portuguese city of 3,400 people that has suffered the fate of many small, rural communities. As young people left in search of opportunity, its population gradually shrank and its economic base eroded. Tourism based on its 500-year history became Castelo de Vide's most important industry. To leverage it for a sustainable future, the city decided to re-connect its economy to the world. It developed a wireless broadband network to serve businesses, citizens and tourists and put its municipal IT into the cloud to reduce costs and expand capabilities. This new infrastructure has made the community more attractive to residents from nearby cities who seek a higher quality of life. It also helped Castelo de Vide attract numerous film and television productions with a unique combination: unspoiled natural beauty to serve as a backdrop for the story, and high-speed broadband to keep production crews connected. Though the

city remains distant from the coastal tourist zone to the west, ICT creates new competitive advantages that serve to close some of the gap.

In 2004, fewer than 6% of Brazilians, or 11 million people, were users of the internet. Of these, about 6% had access to broadband connections, and 90% of them lived in Brazil's biggest cities. Yet, in February of that year, the little city of Pirai, located about 70 kilometers (44 miles) outside Rio de Janeiro and with a population of 23,000, switched on a wireless broadband network providing 14 Mbps of connectivity to every public facility, from the town hall to public schools and street kiosks.

It was an impressive feat of technology implementation. But the technology was the least impressive part.

In 1996, Pirai elected a new mayor, Luiz Fernando de Souza, who felt strongly that communications and information technology should be part of the city's future. The Brasilia University was invited in 1997 to develop an IT master plan for Pirai and, beginning in 2001, the city won a series of grants and loans to plan a "Pirai Digital City" project. Its primary focus was on developing an educational network linking schools, laboratories and libraries, but with the input of donors, it expanded to include efforts to bridge the digital divide with broader coverage. Mayor Souza's government formed an advisory board made up of representatives from government, residential associations, academic and nonprofit organizations, business and labor unions to oversee the continued evolution of the plan.

For several years, funding continued to be both a challenge and opportunity. It was a challenge because the city found it impossible to obtain more grants or loans from the central government to fund deployment of the network. But it was an opportunity because lack of direct funding forced

Pirai to innovate. The city formed alliances with local businesses that could provide expertise, and with a competitive telecommunications company that could help connect nodes in the wireless network. The Pirai branch of CEDERJ, a consortium of public universities offering online courses, agreed to create an Educational Technology Center to oversee implementation. These moves, plus a re-thinking of the network requirements, allowed Pirai to drive down the cost by a factor of eight, and made it possible to finance the project within the city's budget, with only modest assistance from the national government. Through local initiative, Pirai went from one of the least-connected to one of the best-connected places in Latin America in 2004.

The City of Stratford, introduced in previous chapters, offers still other examples. Its largest employer is the Stratford Shakespeare Festival, which attracts cultural tourists from nearby Toronto and much farther beyond. To leverage the Festival's value, Stratford's City Council and the local business community created a public-private Stratford Tourism Alliance.

The Alliance launched advertising campaigns – traditional and online – to make Stratford a destination for "foodies" and cultural tourists. From 2009 to 2010, the Alliance's Internet of Things traffic grew 200% while Ontario Tourism's traffic fell 18% in the financial crisis. More than half of all leisure travelers carry smartphones, and the Alliance introduced a mobile site in 2010 and mobile versions of its "Savor Stratford" Foodies and Festival campaigns. Apps for the iPhone, iPad, Android and BlackBerry followed in 2011, which provided everything from reservations for hotels and restaurants to schedules of events and augmented reality. A set of walking tours of Stratford's many heritage buildings uses signs with QR codes to play 2-3-minute audio clips describing the history of each location.

Stratford is also the center of a four-hospital regional partnership called the Huron-Perth Health Alliance. Its fiber network connects 85% of the physician's groups and family doctors in the Stratford area. The network allows centralized laboratories and specialized care units to serve a widely dispersed set of hospitals, clinics and medical practices, which saves time and money while delivering the highest possible quality of care to a largely rural area. Stratford General Hospital currently conducts 70,000 tests per year for patients in surrounding counties. Physically linked by twice-daily courier, lab results are turned around in hours and, for connected facilities, are available instantly. The interpretation of medical images is likewise centralized, so that four radiologists at the hospital can serve the entire region – with another radiologist in Austria available for off-hours service.

Telemedicine projects include service for mental and emotional conditions that would otherwise need hospitalization. Staff is able to visit clients through a high-quality videoconference to check on their state of mind, ensure they are taking medications and consult on their issues. Client response is overwhelmingly positive: clients see the videoconference terminal not as Big Brother invading their homes but as a tangible sign they are being cared for. Caregivers are equally enthusiastic because eliminating travel time means they can spend more time with clients.

In Stratford's story, we see an attack on all three of the disadvantages of its rural location. A strong online and traditional marketing campaign reaches across distance to attract cultural tourists from throughout the eastern halves of Canada and the US, and deploys the interactivity of social media to foster relationship and keep potential tourists connected to

Stratford's cultural calendar. Within the community, social media apps effectively turn many disparate small businesses into a unified whole in terms of customer marketing. A cultural brand that spans theater, food, history and art projects the charisma that Stratford needs to be a destination not only for tourists but for both companies and employees. And healthcare networking within the greater Stratford region creates the kind of social infrastructure that only dense urban areas are supposed to be able to afford. All have played their part in making Stratford a rural success story.

A little more than a thousand miles (1,700 km) due west of Stratford lies Mitchell, a city of 15,000 on the plains of South Dakota, where it is the center of a region that has lost 30% of its population over the past 70 years. But Mitchell has carved out a sharply different destiny. With a willing private communications company and a Federal broadband stimulus grant, Mitchell has developed a fiber-to-the-premise network serving every business and residence. Its university and technical school have leveraged the city's agricultural heritage into academic leadership in precision agriculture, in which farmers use satellite and remote sensing data to develop a highly detailed portrait of their land and apply that knowledge to boost yields. As part of a strategic plan called Focus 2020, both engage closely with city government, business, primary and secondary schools and a major hospital to promote digital literacy and supply the highly trained workforce in increasing demand by area businesses. These include growing software companies, data centers, customer service centers and communications consulting firms attracted by Mitchell's network or fostered by its construction. Alone in its region, Mitchell has held onto its population and even achieved modest growth. The sheer intensity of its ICT investment, coupled with an effective plan to leverage its other economic assets, has built a new and growing economy on top of its agricultural one.

Private Property for Community Service

A city of 15,000 with its own fiber-to-the-home network is improbable. But then, rural communications has an improbable history. In the US, it dates from 1874, when a man named Joseph Gliddens received, after much effort and acrimony, a patent on his invention of barbed wire. The patent proved enormously valuable, because barbed wire was a rancher's and farmer's dream. On the Great Plains where wood was scarce, barbed wire made it possible to fence off vast tracks of land at a reasonable cost and keep errant cattle and vulnerable crops apart.

What does barbed wire have to do with telecommunications? Two years after the Gliddens patent, Alexander Graham Bell received a patent for his new telephone technology and subsequently formed the Bell Telephone Company to commercialize it. Bell Telephone had things mostly to itself until 1893, when Bell's patents expired. What followed was a competitive scramble by hundreds of upstart companies to wire America's most attractive markets, which then as now were its densely populated and geographically compact cities. Yet by 1912, more farm households than city households had telephones. In 1924, the state with the most telephones per person was not the urbanized states of New York or California but the farm state of Iowa.

How did this come about? One of the virtues of Bell's invention was its simplicity. Connect two telephone handsets to a pair of wires, add electric power from a battery, and you have a workable telephone connection. And that is precisely what thousands of farmers and ranchers did throughout rural America. For a small investment per household, they turned hundreds of miles of barbed wire into telephone networks. These became the basis of rural telephone cooperatives, of which there were some 6,000 across the US in the late 1920s and still many hundreds today. In the words of one observer, it was "private property used for community service."

This principle fueled the earliest forays of rural regions into telecommunications. This principle – that individuals belong to a community with shared interests in maintaining and improving a treasured way of life – is inspiring a new generation of rural leaders. In ways of which we can see only the dim outlines today, they will uncover the models that work, identify the technologies that fit, and give the children of their communities the future they deserve.

CHAPTER NINE

Whatever Happened to the Giant Sucking Sound?

If you lived in America in 1992, you will recognize the words in the title of this chapter, unless you were pursuing spiritual wisdom in a mountaintop cave.

"The giant sucking sound" was the colorful phrase coined by presidential candidate Ross Perot to predict the impact of the North American Free Trade Agreement (NAFTA), which was signed in 1992 and went into force in 1994. It described the sound we would hear as free trade between Canada, the US and Mexico sent good-paying American jobs spiraling down the drain to the lowest-cost outsourcing destination.

Mr. Perot had a gift for making phrases, if not for winning elections. (He received 19% of the popular vote.) The Giant Sucking Sound came to stand for three decades of concern about the offshoring of employment from high-cost zones like the US, Canada and Europe to low-cost zones from Mexico and Eastern Europe to China and Vietnam. In 2010, *The Onion*, a satirical Internet of Things site, mocked these fears with a report that American parents were offshoring child care to India and Sri Lanka, using cardboard boxes to ship their offspring across the seas.

Looking back, it appears that offshoring had devastating impacts on many places from the Seventies through the Nineties. Do a Google search on "offshoring" or "outsourcing" and you will find millions of references to damage done.

As one American blogger put it, "In the 21st century the US economy has been able to create only a few new jobs and these are in lowly paid domestic services that cannot be off-shored, such as waitresses and bartenders...The cause of all of the problems is the offshoring of Americans' jobs. When jobs are moved offshore, consumers' careers and incomes, and the GDP and payroll and income tax base associated with those jobs, go with them...Jobs offshoring is driven by Wall Street, 'shareholder advocates,' the threat of takeovers, and by large retailers such as Walmart. By cutting labor costs, profits go up. It is that simple." [113]

Beginning in 1970, the industrialized nations saw a rapid decline in manufacturing employment. More than 35% of Germans worked in manufacturing in 1970 but fewer than 23% did in 2003. Over the same period, manufacturing employment was halved in Britain and the US, and declined from 25% to 18% even in the manufacturing-intensive Japanese economy.[114]

For every 100 computer manufacturing jobs in the United States in 1950, only 56 remained in 2013. Textiles? From 100 to 31. Apparel? Down to 15.[115] And while the Seventies and Eighties were the heyday of deindustrialization, it has not stopped. A 2007 report from the European Restructuring Monitor attributed 7% of Germany's job losses, 3% of Britain's and a whopping 55% of Portugal's 2005 job losses to offshoring.

The trend got everybody's attention because, throughout the 20th Century, jobs in manufacturing paid lower-skilled workers above-average wages and offered such stability that sons and grandsons followed their fathers into jobs in the same factory. When that many jobs evaporate, particularly those on which the middle class was built, it shatters lives and decimates communities, leaving deep and lasting scars.

During about the same period, developing nations began to grow much faster than they had before. From 1975 to 2001, the advanced economies of the Organization for Economic Cooperation and Development grew their gross domestic products at an average rate of 2.8%. The rate for developing nations was nearly twice that at 4.9%.

During the economic crisis that gripped the world beginning in 2008, Japan saw industrial production drop 15%, the Netherlands 0.8% and the US 0.6% – while China's industrial output *grew* 102%, South Korea's grew 29% and Poland's expanded 21%. [116]

Combine these numbers with decades' worth of news stories about plant closings and decisions to relocate operations to Eastern Europe or Indonesia, and it became clear in most people's minds in the industrialized world that offshoring is sucking the lifeblood from their economies.

There is just one problem with this conclusion. It turns out not to be true.

The Source of the Suck

Take NAFTA. Nearly 20 years after it went into force, politicians, pundits and experts still disagree about its impact. The Economic Policy Institute, a liberal-leaning American think tank, has attributed the loss of about 683,000 US jobs to the agreement through 2010.[117] Others, citing the $12 billion growth in US exports to Mexico and Canada that the agreement helped to foster, estimate that NAFTA has *created* 100,000 jobs. Take your pick. [118]

In 2008, the Globalization and Economic Policy Center at Britain's Nottingham University published a study based on research into 66,000 firms, with particular attention to the 2,850 British multinationals with foreign subsidiaries. The authors looked at the decade from 1994 through 2004, when

UK offshoring increased 35% in manufacturing and 48% in services. Yet in 2005, offshoring still accounted for less than 5% of GDP and 3.5% of all job losses. Companies made more competitive by the market pressure of foreign firms, however, also produced more; the authors calculated that the offshoring surge since the mid-1990s *produced* 100,000 new jobs. [119]

A 2010 paper from the prestigious London School of Economics studied 58 US manufacturing industries from 2000 to 2007 and found that increasing offshore jobs by 1 percent was linked to a 1.72 percent *increase* in overall US employment of native workers. Their conclusion? "Manufacturing industries with a larger increase in global exposure (through offshoring and immigration) fared better than those with lagging exposure in terms of native employment growth." [120]

What's going on? The "offshoring is killing jobs" story is so intuitively believable. Offshoring happens because (greedy) companies in industrialized nations want to take advantage of the low wages paid to workers in developing nations, and because the information and communications (ICT) revolution makes it possible for them to run global operations from the far side of the world.

How could that story be so wrong?

Well, first of all, because it is a simple answer to a complicated question. In 2012, the world's economy was worth about $72 trillion in US dollars. If you live in an industrialized nation, that is more than *two billion times* what the average person makes in a year.[121] It is such a large number, and involves such an incalculable number of activities and decisions, that a red warning light should go off in your mind whenever someone offers you a simple answer about it. The more obvious the conclusion, the more likely it is to be wrong.

Secondly, the ICT revolution does play a role in the loss of manufacturing and, increasingly, service jobs – but it has little to do with those low-wage workers offshore. In 2003, the Gartner Group noticed that the 11% decline in US manufacturing jobs over the previous decade was matched by a 16% decline in Japanese manufacturing employment and a 20% decline in Brazil. "One of the largest losers of manufacturing jobs has been China," Dan Miklovic of Gartner told an audience at the Global Media Summit in November of that year. "We like to pick on China and say that all of these jobs are going to China, but they're losing jobs as well." [122]

If China is not the culprit, who is? Mr. Miklovic has a one-word answer, which is shared by every other expert who has looked seriously at the issue since then.

Automation.

From 1950 to 2010, the percentage of US jobs in the manufacturing sector shrank by two-thirds – but industrial output *grew* by 700%.[123] Would that – could that – have happened if offshoring was the primary causes of shrinking employment?

Let's say you work in a factory producing X units of a widget and the big bosses decide to produce your X units in a factory in Taiwan or Shenzhen. What happens to your job? It disappears from the US and reappears offshore. What happens to the industrial output, those X units you were producing? They disappear from US output and reappear as Taiwanese or Chinese output. Simple, right?

But if US manufacturing output keeps going *up* while the percent of Americans employed in manufacturing keeps going *down*, things are not so simple. Something else is going on: something other than offshoring has to be at work.

What has actually happened is that every industrialized nation has boosted the output of its factories by investing large sums of money in industrial automation. From 2001 to 2011, US industrial output rose 72% for every hour of labor that went into it – not because workers labored so much harder but because machines did an ever-rising portion of the work.[124] Or as Mr. Miklovic of Gartner put it, "We are doing a really good job of improving the productivity of the people." The ones who still have a job, that is.[125]

So, while those shifty-eyed, different-colored foreigners remain an appealing target for blame when it comes to job losses and economic dislocation, the charge just won't stick. No, the truth is a harder pill to swallow.

Despite their overwhelming differences, the people of the world are united in one desire: they want their standard of living to rise over time. They want the future to hold better things for themselves, and they want their children's lives to be better than their own. The list of better things ranges from clean water that does not have to be carried miles by hand in poor nations to better smartphone apps and same-day delivery for online shopping in rich ones.

Whatever the specifics, however, there is only one way to get a better standard of living: by being more productive, which means creating more of what we want using the same or fewer resources. That alone creates economic growth over the long term. If you work in a factory and want to be paid more per hour, the factory has to produce more per hour to provide the money that pays your wage. The big bosses could also get the factory to produce more per hour and not share one penny with you – but basic arithmetic says that they *cannot* pay you more without producing more or being able to charge customers more for what they sell. And it is a rare business these days that can freely raise its prices.

If you accept that premise, it puts the automation issue in a different light. It is not "Wall Street, 'shareholder advocates,' the threat of takeovers, and large retailers such as Walmart" that decimated manufacturing employment in industrialized nations.

It is us.

We demand ever-greater productivity – translated into better stuff at lower prices – and the companies we buy from find a way to deliver it. They do it mostly by investing in automation and information technology. But on the margins, they also send some production offshore to places like Mexico, China and Indonesia that offer much lower labor costs. When a textile mill in the United States or auto assembly plant in Europe closes so that its low-skilled work can shift to a facility in Eastern Europe or Asia, it does represent a siphoning-away of jobs from richer to poorer nations, and it does generate that sucking sound to which Mr. Perot referred. It just does not represent very many of the manufacturing jobs lost. The sucking sound is a lot quieter than expected. And as it turns out, the sibilant siphon can run both ways.

Offshore, Onshore

In August of 2011, the Boston Consulting Group published a report that offered a striking conclusion. Sometime around 2015, it said, manufacturing in the United States will be just as economical as manufacturing in China for many goods that are destined to be sold in North America. [126]

Huh? How is that possible?

Many different factors will contribute to the change, according to BCG. Wages and benefits for the average Chinese factory have been rising at 15-20% per year because demand for semi-skilled labor has outstripped supply. China's labor-cost advantage over low-cost American states is forecast to fall from 55% today to 39% in 2015. And thanks to automation, labor is a shrinking portion of the cost of manufacturing, so the Chinese advantage will ebb even further in real terms. For goods sold into North America, the additional costs of transportation, duties and risks – that the world-circling supply chain will develop kinks – further levels the playing field. Multinational companies will still manufacture in China in vast quantities, but they will be doing it to serve Asian consumers, not North American ones.

The BCG forecast has been controversial, and lots of experts are urging Americans not to break out the champagne just yet. But anecdotal evidence certainly gives industrialized nations a bit of encouragement after many decades of gloom.

NCR moved production of its automated teller machines from offshore to Georgia, where the company expects to create 870 new jobs. An agreement with the United Auto Workers that permits new hires to be paid less motivated Ford to bring 2,000 automotive jobs back to the US. In 2012, General Electric moved manufacturing of home appliances from China to Kentucky. Google has decided to make its media-streaming appliance, Nexus Q, in San Jose. Lenovo, a Chinese tech company, will shortly open a new assembly line for personal computers in Whitsett, North Carolina.

Europe has yet to see a surge in "reshoring," as it is called, but the terrible recession has had the positive result of loosening some labor markets and reducing labor costs, and it could soon happen there as well. [127]

In an industrialized economy like the US, however, manufacturing is no longer a significant employer. Eighty-four percent of Americans worked in service industries in 2010, compared with only 13% in manufacturing and 3% in agriculture and the extraction industries like mining and oil.[128] In the 27 nations of the European Union, the average is 70%

in services, 25% in manufacturing and construction, and 5% in agriculture.

So, what about the outsourcing of services? Many services, from retailing to construction, are inherently local, but others – from call centers and software development to the reading of X-rays – are not, and the same offshoring dynamic began playing out in those services in the first decade of the 21st Century.

According to the always-fallible experts, the future story seems to be the trending the same way. Business services job – in finance, IT and human resources – have been moving offshore from the US and Europe at the rate of 150,000 per year. That figure comes from The Hackett Group, which forecasts that this trend will begin to decline in 2014 and the flow of jobs offshore is likely to cease within 8-10 years.[129]

Why? The grim answer is that the supply of jobs that can be effectively shifted offshore will have grown slim. Hackett estimates that, by 2016, about one third of all US jobs in business services will have moved offshore. The more encouraging answer is that offshoring of both manufacturing and services have proven more of a double-edged sword than many companies expected.

Business executives have learned from hard experience the downside of turning vital parts of their operations over to divisions or other companies on the far side of the world. Doing your engineering and design in one location and your manufacturing in another can save money in the short term – but it robs engineers of expertise in manufacturing, which can wind up costing a lot more money long-term. Handing off key business processes and industrial secrets to another company – or even foreign employees of your own company – risks creating a competitor, particularly in countries where legal protection for intellectual property is weak.

It also turns out that being close to your customers, and ensuring that your key people stay close to what the company does, has enduring value. Location matters. Community matters, even in a global market.

We are fast approaching a time when we must give up our images of the Suck and the Siphon – the one-way or even two-way migration of employment between "us" and them" – in favor of a more complex but realistic picture. Information and communications technology have completely transformed how employers and employees operate in a global economy. And that holds true in both industrialized and emerging market nations.

The View from the Other Side

Industrialized nations have seen the explosive growth of manufacturing on foreign shores as a terrible thing. They have drawn a straight if imaginary line between that growth and the loss of manufacturing in their own countries. But what does it look like from the other side?

In 1950, one year after the Nationalist Kuomintang party, led by Chiang Kai-shek, fled the mainland for Taiwan, the economy of that nation produced $900 per person. That was about 10% of the economic output of each French citizen, 7% of each Australian and 6% of each citizen of the United States. Taiwan was a net recipient of foreign aid, and agriculture made up one-third of the economy. [130]

By 2012, Taiwan's economic output per person had grown to $18,700, which was half that of French citizens, 45% that of Australians and 42% that of Americans. [131] That is an average growth of 6% per year, though good times and bad, which is simply astounding.

This result was the product of what *The Economist* has called "a rare example of successful industrial policy." In

1973, the national government created the Industrial Technology Research Institute (ITRI) to nurture the then-new high-tech industry. ITRI started with semiconductors, those tiny engines of digital innovation, by securing the transfer of patents on old technology from the US company RCA. By 1983, it had developed a clone of the IBM PC and, seven years later, formed an alliance of notebook PC companies.[132]

The authors of this book have all spent time in Taiwan and one recalls walking through a trade fair there in 2004. He was shown a new kind of laptop – one with a touch-sensitive screen and stylus, but no keyboard. It was the size of a small briefcase and weighed about 6 pounds, standard for laptops of that time. After playing with it for a few minutes, he offered the salespeople this forecast. "If you can get this down to the size and weight of a magazine, you will have the killer product of all time."

Well, Steve Jobs at Apple got there first with the iPad. Or so it seems. In 2013, Apple revealed for the first time that, of the 17 factories where its products are assembled and packaged, all but one is owned by a Taiwanese company. Taiwanese companies also make 89% of the world's notebooks as well as 46% of desktop PCs. [133]

Clearly, that kind of growth is good for everybody, and no Taiwanese city shows it more clearly than Taichung, the Intelligent Community of the Year in 2013, which we introduced in a previous chapter. Located in the center of the island at the intersection of a seaport, airport, road and rail networks, Taichung has put tremendous local energy behind the implementation of national policy.

Taichung has a lot of universities, from Feng Chia University with its 21,000 students to Tunghai with 17,000 and Chung Hsing with 16,000. It also has *a lot* of large-scale industrial zones devoted to scientific research, technology development, software and advanced industry. The city is home to 1,500 precision manufacturers, mostly small in scale, as well as thriving food and tourism sectors.

The remarkable thing about Taichung's economy in the 21st Century is the unremitting effort put into making those separate elements work together. Together, the universities operate 13 incubation centers focused on everything from digital technology and biotech to plastics and footwear. A Taichung Incubators Business Alliance nurtures the growth of the more than 400 companies that have graduated from the incubators. City government sponsored an academic-industry training alliance offering training courses in precision machinery, machine tools, mechanical and electrical control and photovoltaic systems, to which 120 manufacturers have sent 800 employees since 2006.

Another city-led initiative created a shared-use ERP platform called the Engineering Data Bank. More than 400 of the city's small precision manufacturers use it to enhance their design, research, development and manufacturing processes. This is the kind of system that only industrial giants can typically afford, and the reduction in rework, errors and delays is now saving these smaller companies a combined total of US$29 million per year.

As for those industrial parks, they are home to just about every kind of technology for which the world has a use. The Central Taiwan Science Park, for example, opened in 2003 and has attracted companies in solar energy, touch-panel displays, optoelectronics, precision chemicals, semi-conductors, aerospace and ICT. In 2011, those companies had combined revenue exceeding US$8.1 billion.

Major success stories include Taiwan Semiconductor Manufacturing Company, a chip foundry that was spun out of ITRI in 1987. With global revenues of US$17.3 billion in

2012, it one of the world's leading silicon chip makers. The company is headquartered in Hsinchu and operates most of its "fabs" there but has massive investment in foundries in Taichung, including a US$10 billion factory in the Central Taiwan Science Park, which employs 8,000 workers. Hon Hai Technology Group (better known as Foxconn) has a US$3.3 billion facility providing R&D and precision machine manufacturing.

All of these companies need logistics, and Taichung's government continuously upgrades its transportation facilities to meet their needs. Taichung Harbor has massive container truck traffic in and out of the port, which requires secure handling and verification. Until 2011, that meant unloading and physically checking cargo, creating a bottleneck that hurt the port's competitiveness. In 2011, Taichung Harbor launched an automatic gate checkpoint system that electronically reads and matches the truck drivers' identification, license plate numbers and container numbers using RFID technology. The entire process takes 2-3 minutes and has proven almost 99% accurate. The savings in time and money for users are enormous and reductions in truck idle time have reduced local air pollution.

Let all of us who live in industrialized nations – with economies turning over trillions of dollars and lifestyles that are the envy of everyone else on the planet – pause for a moment to consider Taichung and the greater island of Taiwan. *This is what a people do when they believe in a better future.* They combine the resources of business, government and institutions, each limited in its own way, to make massive investments in infrastructure and the means to operate it.

In the 21st Century, the infrastructure of most rich nations is slowly eroding for lack of that investment. In 2009, the American Society of Civil Engineers (ASCE) estimated that the nation needed to spend at least $2.2 trillion over the next five years to repair its infrastructure.[134] So, five years later, how was the nation doing? The 2013 ASCE report card foresaw the need to spend *$3.6 trillion* by 2020 – but estimated that only $2 trillion worth of projects was on the drawing board.[135]

Even Germany, that exemplar of efficiency, has skimped on maintenance. A government commission concluded in 2013 that the country needs to spend $138 billion over the next 15 years to get existing infrastructure back into shape.

When we believe that the future holds a greater chance of gain than loss, we invest in our own future and that of our children. When we believe the opposite, we invest in today's rewards. So those of us who live in the rich nations of the world should ask ourselves: what kind of future do we truly believe in?

Taichung makes a great study in forward-looking collaboration among government, business and universities to drive growth of its manufacturing sector. But Taichung's economy is not really about manufacturing. According to the city's Economic Development Bureau, services account for 70% of Taichung's economic output: restaurants and catering, retailing, accommodations, culture, tourism, meetings and conferences. That makes it a thoroughly modern industrial economy. [136]

And yet the same restless desire to innovate and improve is at work here. Agriculture is now only 5% of the economy, for example, but Taichung's institutes have created a Biotechnology Farm. Here are applied the principles of semiconductor clean rooms to boost the output of mushroom farming by a factor of four. Similarly advanced methods have boosted tomato production 10-fold. A one-year marketing push by the city's Bureau of Agriculture boosted agricultural exports throughout Asia 63% from 2010 to 2011.

It is a good thing that Taichung's economy is so diverse – and that the city works hard to keep its many sectors competitive. Because the Giant Sucking Sound can be heard over Taichung as well. Remember those 17 factories in which the iPad is manufactured, 16 of them owned by Taiwanese companies? The Taiwanese may own them but 14 of the factories are in mainland China, where a steady supply of cheap migrant labor, eager to escape grinding rural poverty, has fed the massive manufacturing facilities. Overall, 98% of ICT hardware manufactured by Taiwanese companies today is actually made in China. With Chinese costs rising, Terry Guo, the CEO of Hon Hai Technology (aka Foxconn), has vowed to build one million robots to shift his factories to near 100% automation. As a side benefit, he predicts that manufacture of his "Foxbots" will become an important line of business in the future.[137]

A Talent for Adaptation

With this kind of innovative competition, how do the economic leaders of the 20th Century continue to offer their people a prosperous future in the 21st? A talent for adaptation is clearly required, and no city shows that better than Oulu, Finland, a city of 188,000 located 200 km south of the Arctic Circle, which we introduced in Chapter Three.

If you have never heard of it, you don't work in the wireless industry. Oulu was a Top7 Intelligent Community in both 2012 and 2013. As part of the Intelligent Community Awards program, ICF co-founders visit each of the Top7. And on one such visit, one of the authors was taken to visit a Nokia manufacturing plant.

Nokia has been through some rough years. In 2003, the company sold 35% of all mobile phones. By June of 2013, its market share of handsets was down to less than 4%, and the company chose to sell its handset business to Microsoft, while retaining its mobile infrastructure business.[138]

For decades, Nokia has been an anchor employer in Oulu. In 1990, the Nokia Research Center and its SME vendors were the city's most important employers. The restructuring and layoffs that accompanied its downturn hit Oulu hard.

The visit to that plant, which makes wireless base station equipment, revealed a talent for adaptation that points the way for cities around the world. This facility exists to take prototypes of new equipment and turn them into production models. Its production capacity is deliberately limited to the thousands of units. Once they have worked out all the bugs and found the most efficient way to produce the product, manufacturing moves to Asia, where contract manufacturers make millions of them at per-unit costs that the Nokia plant could never equal.

But the Oulu plant is not out of the loop. It also functions as the repair facility for the equipment it helps create. Everything that fails in the field comes back to Oulu, where it is tested, torn down and diagnosed. The lessons learned go into product upgrades, which are put through the plant's processes until they are ready to go to Asia and be implemented in mass manufacturing.

Most of the personnel in the plant are highly skilled, from engineers to technicians to design specialists. Sure, there are lower-skilled jobs as well. The factory has, believe it or not, five saunas for employees, and somebody has to maintain them. But it is clear in Oulu, as in most innovative economies, that economic rewards flow to those with abstract knowledge and practical skills.

When the plant needs to do a production run, management hires engineering and technology students from the University of Oulu to work part time. The young people appreciate the money and the chance to see high-tech manufacturing first-hand. Nokia gets products into the hands of customers faster and can make sure those products work properly before committing to high-volume production. And the benefits run like a river through the economy of Oulu.

For Oulu did not waste the long period of Nokia's prosperity. Working in collaboration with its university, the city made itself a global center of excellence in wireless communications. The university launched a Center for Wireless Communications in 1995, which has produced a steady stream of "firsts" in mobile voice and data using funding from industry and government. Four other centers of excellence have been created since then, focusing on intelligent systems, internet usability and health. Every year, organizations in Oulu are granted 500 new patents and 400 new companies get their start. Elektrobit, founded in Oulu in 1985, now employs 1,600 people in seven countries, developing wireless technologies and advanced embedded electronics for the automobile industry. A much younger company, Codenomicon, provides tools for the automated testing of network protocols for companies including Microsoft, Sony-Ericsson and Nokia Siemens Networks.

The stories of Taichung and Oulu teach the same lesson: it is no longer about us and them, about blaming people in faraway lands for the seismic changes sweeping the places we live, work and pursue our dreams. We are all in the same boat, rocked by the same waves of dynamic change made possible by a hyperconnected world.

Modern economies prosper from being specialized. Some of the food that farmers grow feeds insurance brokers who sell them crop insurance. By specializing in different things, both do better than if they tried to do everything themselves. The way to be a successful community – whether in industrialized or developing nations – is to figure out what you are good at and then commit to having the people, infrastructure and innovation capacity to deliver it. And when what you are good at is no longer in high demand, to figure out what your next specialization will be.

Today, more than ever before in history, employment flows to where the brains are – to places with the appropriate level of skills for the job, places where collaboration is a way of life, and places with the physical and digital infrastructure needed for success. In short, to Intelligent Communities.

CHAPTER TEN

Strangers in a Strange Land

Why should Pennsylvania, founded by the English, become a Colony of Aliens, who will shortly be so numerous as to Germanize us instead of our Anglifying them, and will never adopt our Language or Customs, any more than they can acquire our Complexion?[139]

So wrote no less an innovator and champion of liberty than Benjamin Franklin. It was in the days before his storied career as revolutionary, signer of America's Declaration of Independence, framer of the US Constitution and America's first Minister to France and Sweden. In a 1751 essay, Franklin complained about how many German settlers were congregating in his native state. Yet in this same essay, he noted how little of that state's vast expanse of fertile land had been put to use and he promoted agriculture as a means of self-advancement. "No man continues long a laborer for others," he wrote, "but gets a plantation of his own."

In that single essay by a Founding Father, we find the twin responses of the native-born to immigration, as common in Franklin's time as in our own.

We need and want the labor, vitality and ambition brought to us by immigrants, who frequently risk all on the chance of finding a better life.

We fear and loathe the immigrants themselves because they speak a different language, look different from us and have different ways of life.

These responses, linked as closely as our minds and hearts, offer a challenge to every city and region in the world. They are like opposite poles of a magnet, one of which seeks to attract immigrants while the other seeks to repel them. In a world where global interconnectedness is determining the economic destiny of the places we live, your community's position between those poles matters. At one end lies the opportunity to gain the world's best brains to power your economy, enrich your society and expand your culture. At the other lies the threat of seeing your own best brains drained to places where they find a warmer welcome.

Two of the authors of this book are the grandchildren of immigrants. One is an immigrant himself. He can still remember his arrival on a stormy December day in 1955, at the age of four, when the captain of the *General W.C. Langfitt* decided to brave the entrance to New York City's crowded harbor despite the bad weather. He recalls the taste of salt and shoreline in the air and his first sight of the Statue of Liberty, with her invitation to "the wretched refuse of your teeming shores," and the mighty towers of Manhattan nearby. The boy saw tears of joy in the eyes of the immigrants crowding the deck that day, and felt the anxiety rippling just beneath the surface as they contemplated the new world they were about to enter. His people, the Jungs, were Germans – of the same stock whose numbers had so upset Dr. Franklin in 1751 – and they were fleeing their war-devastated land for the opportunities to be found in the world's one nation that emerged from war more powerful and prosperous than ever.

Welcoming the Wretched Refuse

Its infrastructure untouched by bombing and its industrial muscle grown mighty with wartime production, America was bursting with opportunity. Immigration programs were encouraging people to come from across the seas to help power more growth, and immigrants who found success were telling their relatives back home about this limitless land of milk and honey.

After getting their bearings in New York, German immigrants moved onward to Kansas to work on the wheat farms and to Texas to work in industry. They found employment in the automotive plants of Detroit and the breweries of Milwaukee, Wisconsin and Columbus, Ohio, where they joined the previous wave of German immigrants, who had come to the US between 1848 and the First World War, fleeing revolutions in their homeland.[140]

The Jung family went instead to the state of New York. After a brief stay in New York City – where young John Jung endured teasing as a DP or "displaced person" in kindergarten – the family moved north and the elder Mr. Jung found work at Bethlehem Steel in Lackawanna, just south of the city of Buffalo. It was an attractive spot, a city that had known strong growth since the completion of the Erie Canal in 1825, but unknown to the Jungs, it was on the threshold of decades of steady decline.

The choice of destination was no accident. Immigrants then as now tended to cluster where their relatives had established a beachhead. Greeting the Jung family at Pier 42 in Manhattan was an uncle who had made the crossing with his family years before. It was his letters that encouraged John's father to bring his family to America. It was the uncle who persuaded William Miller, a New York politician of German descent who would be the running mate of the Republican presidential hopeful Barry Goldwater in 1964, to be the Jungs' guarantor.

They settled in a community called Black Rock on the Canadian border, where it was common to hear German spoken in the streets. Learning the English of their new country was easy for young John and his siblings but remained a daunting barrier to their parents. In the ancient pattern of immigration everywhere, the parents' years of menial labor at the steel mill and cleaning houses gave their children the opportunity for education and the prospect of a more prosperous life than their own. From this community of immigrants and urban poor, the family moved upward, and the descendants of the eldest Jungs became lawyers, doctors, engineers and teachers, each adding to the economic and social progress of the places they chose to live.

The Jung family saga captures the positive story of immigration for the nations and the local communities where immigrants settle. Immigration remains deeply controversial in most countries, but a strong body of evidence suggests that its impact is overwhelmingly positive.

A 2013 study, conducted by Duke University for the Partnership for a New American Economy, assessed the economic impact of immigration on more than 3,000 US counties between 1970 and 2010. It found that immigrants contribute by earning and spending money, benefiting local business, and by generating tax revenues. They also provide companies with a pool of workers whose skills are in short supply in the broader US population.[141]

"For every 1,000 immigrants who live in a county," said Jeremy Robbins, director of the Partnership, "46 manufacturing jobs are created or preserved." Manufacturing is not the only beneficiary. For every 1,000 immigrants that move into an area, the study found, 270 native-born people also come, as small businesses are launched to serve the growing demand for services.

"Immigration yields a significant impact on home values across the country, occurring most notably in relatively affordable metropolitan areas and neighborhoods," according to the report.

Other studies support these findings. Nigerians make up less than 1 percent of the black population of the United States but, in 2013, nearly one-quarter of the black students at Harvard Business School. Over one-fourth of Nigerian-Americans have a graduate or professional degree compared with about 11 percent of whites.[142]

It is easy to see how immigrants themselves benefit from immigration. What we tend to forget is that their increasing prosperity ripples through the economy and benefits everyone else as well. A 2006 paper by two economists concluded that immigration since 1990 has boosted the average wage of native-born Americans by between 0.7% and 1.8%.[143] Fully 90% of US native-born workers are estimated to have gained from immigration, and a quick bit of math – multiplying the average percent gain by the total wages of US native workers – suggests that the native-born saw total wage gains of between $30 and $80 billion.[144]

Why are immigrants such good news? The Kaufman Foundation in the US has found that their index of entrepreneurial activity is 40% higher than that of natives.[145] In other words, they start businesses, from dry-cleaning to construction to automotive repair, that employ people and create new household income. Jason Nguyễn arrived in Oakland, California with his wife and two small children in 1997, after a perilous journey from Vietnam. The rickety boat on which they escaped that country managed to stay afloat until its passengers were rescued by a freighter that took them to Hong Kong, from which the Nguyễns traveled to America. Jason could not speak or write English, but he found work in the garlic fields of Gilroy in the Santa Clara Valley, and he and his wife eventually started their own vegetable and floral business in Oakland. Today, the children of these "boat people" are Robert Nguyễn, a well-regarded orthopedic surgeon, and Sally Nguyễn, an Oakland Councilwoman.

In 2011, immigrants started 28 percent of all new US businesses and employed one in ten American workers. In New York City, which initially welcomed the Jung family, job creation in immigrant neighborhoods was almost three times the city average.[146]

And it is not all corner fruit stands and taxi cabs. In the US, immigrants generated twice the number of patents of native-born filers over the past decade, and created 25% of the technology and engineering firms in the US, employing over 450,000 people and generating over $52 billion in sales.

Google's Co-founder, Sergey Brin was born in Moscow but attended Stanford University, where he met Larry Page and launched Google in 1998. Andrew Grove, born in Budapest, is the co-founder of Intel. German-born Andreas von Bechtolsheim and Indian–born Vinod Khosla joined forces with fellow Stanford alumnus Scott McNealy and Bill Joy in 1982 to form Sun Microsystems. Taiwanese-born Jerry Yang is the Co-founder of Yahoo! In Canada, Turkish-born Mike Lazaridis co-founded BlackBerry and Hungarian Peter Munk founded Barrick Gold, the world's largest gold-mining firm.

Immigrants tend to contribute more to such entitlement programs as Social Security (government-funded pensions) and Medicare (health insurance for the elderly) than they receive. But as the list of technology pioneers suggests, the biggest payoff comes over time. A study by America's National Research Council found that the average immigrant, including descendants, contributes about $80,000 more in taxes than he or she receives in public services. The surplus is larger for higher-skilled immigrants ($198,000) and turns into a deficit of -$13,000 for less-skilled workers.[147]

Why are immigrants so often successful? According to Amy Chua and Jed Rubenfeld, writing in *The New York Times*:

Group success in America often tends to dissipate after two generations. Thus while Asian-American kids overall had SAT scores 143 points above average in 2012 — including a 63-point edge over whites — a 2005 study of over 20,000 adolescents found that third-generation Asian-American students performed no better academically than white students.

It turns out that for all their diversity, the strikingly successful groups in America today share three traits that, together, propel success. The first is a superiority complex — a deep-seated belief in their exceptionality. The second appears to be the opposite — insecurity, a feeling that you or what you've done is not good enough. The third is impulse control.[148]

America has been on the receiving end of immigration since the Massasoit tribe of Massachusetts made the mistake of not driving the Pilgrims back into the sea. But its impacts are similar around the world. The UK's Centre for Economics and Business Research concluded in 2013 that immigration from the European Union contributes £20 billion (US$33bn) to the British economy, and that migrants were more likely to have a job than the average UK-born citizen. Celebrity chef Jamie Oliver got into hot water in August of that year with a much publicized claim that EU immigrants have a better work ethic than the British.[149]

A study by the London School of Economics identified two benefits arising from a doubling of London's foreign-born population over 20 years to 2 million people. Immigration improved the diversity, flexibility, international experience and skill sets of London's workforce. It also expanded the labor supply, which helped drive employment growth while reducing upward pressure on wages.[150] Britain's foreign-born population includes a higher proportion of people with higher education than any nation except Canada, and more of them are in the one-tenth of the population earning the highest incomes than in any nation except Australia.[151]

A 2013 report from the Organization for Economic Cooperation and Development (OECD) examined the fiscal impact of immigrants in 27 rich countries. Despite concern that immigrants soak up far more government spending than they contribute in tax revenue, the study found a generally positive impact on national budgets equal to an average of 0.3% of GDP from 2007 to 2009. The highest contribution was not in the United States but in Luxembourg (0.37% of GDP), while Germany saw the biggest shortfall (-1.93% of GDP), due to the larger number of elderly pensioners who came from Turkey as guest workers in the 1960s.[152]

Let Them Stay Where They Are

So, if immigrants are good news for the countries that receive them, why is immigration such a source of strife? The British recoil from Polish plumbers and roving Bulgarians. Australians fight to keep boat people from a half-dozen Asian nations off their shores. Germans grumble about Turks, Italians sing arias of outrage over immigrants from the Middle East and Africa, while Americans want everyone south of the Rio Grande to stay where they are. And the Japanese – afflicted with a shrinking workforce, minimal birthrate and deflation – have been so successful at keeping out immigrants that less than 2% of Japan's population is foreign-born.[153]

A 2013 online poll by Harris Interactive asked people in Britain, France, Germany, Italy, Spain and the US what they thought about immigration. Sixty-four percent of Britons said that it made their country a worse place to live, followed by 60% in Spain, 57% in Italy, 49% in the US, 44% in Germany and 43% in France. Sixty-seven percent of Spaniards said that immigration made it harder to find a job, compared with 45% in France.[154]

Drill down into these numbers and the list of immigrant offenses is long. They commit crimes. They are "welfare tourists" shopping for a new homeland offering the best deal on public assistance. When they do work, their eagerness to accept lower wages steals jobs from us or makes the jobs we do have pay less. They refuse to integrate and become like us – instead, they try to force their foreign ways onto us in the form of signs in shop windows, new kinds of foods in the grocery store and new ways to worship. They are lazy, smelly, dirty and carriers of disease.

The fact that almost none of this is true does not seem to matter. A 2012 study from America's respected Pew Research Center found that, in rural counties that experienced an influx of immigrants in the Eighties and Nineties, crime rates *dropped* by more than they did in rural counties that did not see high immigrant growth. Immigrant youths in Los Angeles were less involved in crime and violence than their native-born peers.[155]

It does not matter because we *feel* it. Deep down in the unreasoning parts of ourselves, we *know* it to be true regardless of what experts and statistics tell us.

In this respect, we are true to our ancestry. Like the apes from which we descend, human beings are intensely tribal. We like what we know and are deeply comforted by the familiar. We identify ourselves with the signs and symbols of our tribe, be it a football team's logo or a particular style of wearing a burnoose. And when we encounter those who are clearly not part of our tribe, our first response is anxiety and aggression. We are naturally suspicious of the stranger in our midst and are vigilant for the smallest sign that he is a danger to us. It has been this way for the 10,000 years of human history and – at the level of the cerebellum and other unreasoning parts – it is unlikely to change.

To be fair, not all of this anxiety and aggression is without foundation. The last few pages of statistics have one thing in common: they speak to the impact of immigrants on entire nations or groups of nations like the European Union. When we narrow our focus to a smaller region or individual city, a high volume of immigration is not always good news.

Remember that National Research Council study, which shows an average long-term gain of $80,000 in taxes for individual immigrants and their descendants? It noted that, for less-skilled immigrants, that surplus is actually a deficit of -$13,000. That may not be so bad when spread across a nation's population. But if your particular city or region is being flooded by low-skilled immigrants, they are probably a drain on public finances rather than a boon.

The London School of Economics study of economic impacts in London found a similar result in terms of salaries. A concentration of immigrants in the worst-paid segment of the workforce, it found, produced a significant downward pressure on wages at the bottom end of the market. Reduced wages had the positive effect of encouraging job growth (lower prices tend to increase demand) but caused earnings for workers to fall behind growth in the cost of living. So, if your community or region has a lot of low-wage jobs and an influx of immigrants, household earnings may be caught in a race for the bottom.[156]

While wages downshift, costs can move in the opposite direction. Any growth in population tends to raise costs temporarily, because more demand is chasing the same amount of supply, until the market responds by increasing that supply. The gain in the value of housing identified by the Duke University study is great for people who own their own homes already. But for renters and first-time home buyers, it represents growth in the single largest cost of living.

For all these reasons, the hot spots for contention over immigration are usually at the borders where immigrants congregate before dispersing across nations. In the United States, it is the border with Mexico, where the least-skilled immigrants enter the country legally or not. In Europe, it is in Greece, Italy and Spain, whose coastlines are the target of migrants from the turbulent Middle East and Africa. For Turkey, it is the borders with Syria and Iraq, both wracked by Sunni-Shiite violence in the second decade of the 21st Century.

The travails of those places are real, though hardly the fault of the destitute and bewildered immigrants who wash up on their shore. Yet there are also places where wave after wave of immigrants have arrived and, with the odd exception, been well integrated into the social order. More than 50 cities around the world are now the students of the immigration policies of the City of New York, under Fatima Shama, commissioner for immigrant affairs. She was appointed in 2009 by Mayor Michael Bloomberg, who had already issued executive orders allowing all immigrants access to city services and shielding them from questions about their legal status when reporting crimes.[157]

Ms. Shama, the daughter of immigrants from Palestine and Brazil, added educational campaigns to combat immigration fraud, improve healthcare access and encourage immigrants to learn English and gain financial literacy. Policies promoted immigrant businesses and the training of new community leaders in immigrant neighborhoods. She also left a legacy for cities around the world by publishing her office's strategy in a set of documents called *Blueprints for Immigrant Innovation.* [158]

The city's bet on the value of immigration has paid off handsomely. Immigrants accounted for US$215 billion in economic activity in 2008, nearly one third of the city's GDP. They made up 36% of the city's population but 43% of its workforce. Their share of the workforce grew by 68%, their wages by 39% and their contribution to the city's economy by 61% from 2000 to 2008. The ten neighborhoods with the greatest concentration of immigrants had stronger economic growth than the rest of the city and saw the number of businesses grow by four times the city average.[159]

Putting Out the Welcome Mat

National governments are in charge of immigration policy, because they are responsible for the country's borders. Yet the impact of that policy is felt most acutely at the local level, where every member of the nation lives, works and helps raise the next generation. Whatever the current debate in your nation, it turns out that your city or region has a choice. And there are few issues where the right choice is so crystal clear.

Your community cannot do much about immigration itself, any more than you can direct the vast energies of the global economy that is driven by the broadband revolution. Like it or not, you are on the receiving end, and if immigrants find your community desirable for any of a dozen reasons, come they will, whether you want them or not. The choice your community faces is simple. You can work to help immigrants integrate and succeed, so that your community reaps the greatest benefit from their presence. Or you can resist with all your might and thereby ensure that you receive all of the costs and few of the gains.

If this sounds familiar, that is because the community's choices on immigration so closely resemble its choices on all the other changes wrought by the Broadband Economy. You can either adopt and adapt – placing your faith in a new future – or you can resist, resign and stagnate.

The choice is easily stated but can be hard to make. Learning to welcome immigrants is not easy. It takes a mix of the right attitude and the right practices, both of which may take a good deal of time and effort to develop.

Columbus Mayor Michael Coleman won election for the first time in 1999 on a pledge to create 10,000 new housing units and transform a city that had lost its economic and social momentum. The de-industrialization of the 1970s and 1980s contributed to it. So did poor urban planning: high construction cut off several low-income neighborhoods from the city center, which led to sharp population declines there that left swathes of derelict housing while the overall population of Columbus remained stable.

The new administration took steps that would be recognizable to any imaginative economic developer. It worked to attract and support commercial developers to the downtown core, where new office buildings and public facilities gradually transformed the skyline. The Mayor also closed deals with commercial residential developers to build condominiums in place of derelict housing. When the financial crisis struck in 2008-09, the city committed large sums to buy and either demolish or start maintaining derelict properties to prevent further decay.

But one of Mayor Coleman's first acts was convene a group of local business leaders and lead them on a mission to Toronto, Canada. He wanted them to see first-hand what that city had done to make itself a magnet for immigration, and the positive impact the new citizens had had on its economy. The

Mayor believed that immigration, properly channeled, was a key to Columbus's economic future and the re-energizing of its culture. He was persuasive enough that the business leaders – who were to form the core of a permanent public-private policy group called the Columbus Partnership – returned home convinced of this vision and ready to work on its implementation.

Back at home, Mayor Coleman established a program called the New American Initiative, which aimed to give all immigrants living in Columbus access to services that would improve their lives. Its programs are designed to tackle the challenges of language, education, affordable housing, healthcare and employment. Rather than operating as a standalone program, the Initiative provides a specialized focus on immigrants within the city's community relations department. These include Community Intervention Teams from the police and fire departments, which work with community leaders to build trusting relationships. A Community Relations Commission is empowered to investigate and resolve complaints about discrimination, and conducts cultural sensitivity training for community groups, businesses and institutions throughout the city.

This labor has not gone unrewarded. In a recent survey, the city asked Columbus residents to provide adjectives to describe their city. The two most frequently cited were "smart" and "open." That helps to explain why, today, Columbus is home to America's largest Somali population and a fast-growing group of Mexican immigrants. In the state of Ohio, of which Columbus is the capital, immigrants have accounted for 72% of population growth since 2000. More than half have arrived in the past 10 years. The central Ohio region now ranks second in the United States for the percentage of new foreign-born residents. According to an editorial in *The Columbus Dispatch*, "In 2012, the purchasing power of Ohio Latinos reached $8.2 billion and that of Ohio Asians $9.7 billion, both more than a 400 percent increase. Asian-owned businesses supported more than 50,000 jobs, and Latino-owned companies more than 11,500." [160]

How to Grow a City

For communities in the industrialized world, immigration can be the only thing standing in the way of population decline. The baby boom generation that followed World War II is aging out of the economy, and the birthrate in most rich nations is below the level needed to sustain the population they have.

Eindhoven, the high-tech manufacturing hub of the Netherlands, is vitally aware of the challenge. In 2013, *Forbes* named it the world's most inventive city, and its companies face a growing shortage of skilled labor to keep the innovation engine turning. The region's cooperative economic development agency, Brainport Development, has created many different programs to draw talented people from around the world to Eindhoven.

The Brainport Talent Center is a partnership of businesses, educational and research institutions and the regional government of southeastern Holland. It focuses on attracting and retaining experienced and skilled tech employees from within and outside the Netherlands. Its primary project is a shared talent pool that employers can tap for internships, consulting assignments and full-time employment at all educational levels.

The Taskforce Technology, Education and Employment program (abbreviated TTOA in Dutch) focuses on promoting the interest of young people in engineering, attracting foreign knowledge workers, and on career counseling and lifelong learning. TTOA goes on the road to international career fairs in the US, Europe, Turkey, India and China to promote opportunities in the Eindhoven region. Its Expatguideholland.com Internet of Things site provides information and services to smooth the path of highly skilled immigrants and their families.

This focus on immigration-fueled development goes right to the top. In January 2014, Eindhoven's appointed Mayor, Rob van Gijzel, delivered a speech criticizing the Dutch government for lack of vision. "More than other countries," he said, "the Netherlands keeps its borders as closed as possible or discourages people from coming here. If this does not change, the economy will be put back by years."[161] To counter that trend, Mayor van Gijzel travels the world to establish bilateral relationships with other technology hubs, seeking opportunities for Eindhoven companies to develop strategic partnerships and exchange skilled employees. In 2013, Eindhoven entered such a relationship with Waterloo in Canada, which connected the 2011 Intelligent Community of the Year with its 2007 predecessor.

Canada has long encouraged immigration to meet the economic needs of a nation with far more resource-rich land than people to occupy it. From 2002 to 2011, every Canadian province or territory except Ontario saw immigration rise by between two and seventeen times.[162] According to the Conference Board of Canada's new report, *The Influence of Immigrants on Trade Diversification in Saskatchewan*, the more immigrants a province has, the more the economy is able to grow. The report investigated the correlation between trade and immigrant levels and suggested that "for every one percent increase in immigration levels, there is a $30 million increase in imports and $41 million increase in exports."[163]

In recent years, national and provincial policies have focused on attracting highly skilled immigrants to power innovation-based economic growth. A study called *Immigrants as Innovators: Boosting Canada's Global Competitiveness* reports that immigrants are a significant part of Canada's productivity and innovation, critical for a country's economic development. The report indicates that "at every level of analysis, immigrants are shown to have an impact on innovation performance that is benefiting Canada."

According to the study, 35 percent of 1,800 Canada Research Chairs are foreign-born, even though immigrants are just one-fifth of the Canadian population. For instance, Guang Jun Liu arrived in Toronto from China in 1990 with a master's degree in robotics. Today, he is the Canada Research Chair in control systems and robotics at Ryerson University, who also works with such groups as the Canadian Space Agency. Liu is living proof of how immigrants can help boost Canada's stature in innovation.[164]

Getting to this point of actively welcoming the strangers has been a long road. According to an April 2013 article in *Maclean's*, Canada has excelled at attracting skilled immigrants but does not quite know what to do with them once they are settled in their new country. "In 1970," wrote journalist Tamsin McMahon, "men who immigrated to Canada earned about 85% of the wages of Canadian-born workers, rising to 92% after a decade in the country. By the late 1990s, they earned just 60%, rising to 78% after 15 years." The problem, McMahon posits, is that immigration policy has been almost too successful, creating a surplus of talented immigrants competing for jobs. Today, university-educated immigrants earn an average of 67% of their native-born peers. As a result, nearly half of chronically poor immigrants living in Canada were classified as skilled workers upon arrival."[165]

While such temporary imbalances are a problem, Canada has clearly been successful at the immensely difficult task of welcoming the stranger.   A recent study suggests that Canadians have grown more tolerant even though the number of foreigners entering Canada has increased over the years. The Institute for Research on Public Policy found 58% of Canadians supported the country's level of immigration over the past decade – about the same percentage of British and American citizens who think there are too *many* immigrants in their country.[166] A German Marshall Fund poll also found that Canadians were more tolerant of immigrants than surveys taken in the U.S. and throughout Europe, such as Germany, Italy, France, Spain, Netherlands and Scandinavia.[167]

Canadians did not always have this positive view. The shift took place over a decade ago through education and promotion of multiculturalism as a national source of pride and bringer of economic and social benefits.

The good news, then, is that we can be taught to ignore the lures of our unreasoning tribalism and embrace the stranger in our midst. Toronto, Canada's financial capital and biggest city, was a role model for Columbus Mayor Coleman and remains so today. More than 52% of its population was born in another country. The city boasts the largest population of Italians outside of Italy and largest cluster of Chinese in North America. Evidence of Toronto's multiculturalism is everywhere from street signs and ethnic media to neighborhood festivals enlivening its streets and event halls. The Toronto region is expected to grow by 50% through 2031, with immigration the largest contributor.

The need to get local immigration policy correct was dramatized by the story of Sanjay Mavinkurve and his wife

Samvita Padukone. An engineer born in India and raised in Saudi Arabia, Sanjay was working for Google in Silicon Valley when he married Samvita in 2008. She had a job in finance with Singapore's largest investment bank, but her new husband's temporary visa did not allow her to work in the US. So, Google transferred Sanjay to its Toronto office, where Canadian immigration policy welcomed his highly educated and experienced wife.

The Canadian media loved it and published pictures of the young couple sitting on the couch of their downtown Toronto apartment, smiling beneath a Canadian flag.

To her shock, however, Samvita found it impossible to find work. Calls to employers went unreturned or recruiters told her that she would need Canadian work experience to qualify. In 2009, after Samvita received a US work visa, the couple moved south of the border to Seattle, where she won the first job she applied for, at Amazon's headquarters.[168]

To counter the kind of barriers that made Samvita's year in Toronto so frustrating, the city operates programs like the Immigrant Employment Data Initiative. It partners with immigration service agencies, employer associations, regulatory bodies, training organizations and professional credentialing groups. It amasses data on immigration trends, ethnic diversity, adult literacy and skills, and other factors that help these partner agencies set sensible policies to integrate the immigrant population.

The city's Immigration Portal offers in-depth guidance for immigrants before and after they arrive on applying for residency, city services, finding a home, job opportunities and education. A City Mentorship Program helps immigrants with professional credentials from foreign nations, like physicians or engineers, with the daunting task of finding suitable work in their fields.

There are even neighborhood-based projects: the Toronto South Local Immigration Partnership is one of several that helps newcomers find housing, find a job, learn English and deal with the challenges that come with living in a different society and culture.[169]

The city solidified its immigrant-friendly reputation in February 2013, when the City Council approved a motion designating Toronto as a Sanctuary City, one of more than 30 across North America including New York City. Sanctuary Cities provide all municipal services without regard to immigration status and bar law enforcement from inquiring about immigration status as part of their investigations.

The Never-Ending Story

The Jung family immigration saga did not end with the family's arrival in Black Rock, New York, USA. Following the death of his father at a relatively early age, John Jung's mother was married again, this time to a Canadian. His elder siblings were adults and elected to stay in the US, but John was still short of his majority and went with his mother to a new home north of the border.

With family on both sides of the line, John was a regular international traveler. He had been born in Germany, spent years as a legal US immigrant and now lived in Canada – all of which made him a walking red flag for US Immigration, particularly at a time when young American men were moving north to avoid being drafted into the military for service in Vietnam. Every crossing meant endless questions from people in uniform and frequently ended with him being turned back into Canada. Once, on a university trip into the US, officials held his entire party of students and professors for four hours before granting entry.

His final choice of country was determined by love. Marrying a Canadian, he applied for citizenship and received the Canadian passport which ended his trials with US Immigration. In the time since, he has made his own innovative contributions to urban planning and economic development with governments and regional agencies across Canada.

But a certain restless appears to have been handed down in the blood. The next generation of Jungs have lived and worked in several countries and one son has emigrated, at least for now, to Australia.

The global economy, forged by information and communications technology, is penetrating deeper into every city and region, year after year. Its inevitable partner is immigration, as the flow of digital bits is followed by a matching flow of bodies and souls. In the decades ahead, the communities that truly welcome them, regardless of the obstacles, will be the ones that prove their intelligence.

Brain Gain

CHAPTER ELEVEN

How to Save Your City...and Still Win the Next Election

In Amsterdam, you can work for the public sector and get paid in beer.

Well, not only in beer. Each member of several street-cleaning teams in the Dutch capital also receives a half packet of rolling tobacco, free lunch and 10 Euros a day. But they start work at 9 am with two cans of beer, down two more at lunch and one more at the end of the workday.

For these workers, the beer is the great attractor. They are employed by the Rainbow Foundation, a government-funded organization that helps alcoholics, substance abusers and the homeless get back on their feet. In three districts of Amsterdam, long-term alcoholics clean the streets in return for their liquid salary, giving back while giving in to temptation. "I'm not proud to be an alcoholic," Fred Schiporst, a former construction worker, told *The New York Times*, "but I am proud to have a job again."[170]

Even in the Netherlands, known for its tolerance of lifestyle differences, the program is controversial. Members of Council have called it misguided and a waste of government money. But a district mayor, Fatima Elatik, supports the program even though she is a Muslim whose faith outlaws the drinking of alcohol. It is better, she said, to give them something useful to do than simply to ostracize them.

Let's take a moment for a thought experiment. Imagine yourself in your own country, at a public meeting in your own city or town, giving a speech in which you urge local government to take a page from Amsterdam's book and put alcoholics on the public payroll, payable in the products of fermentation.

Depending on where you live, it could be a very short speech. In most places, this kind of program would be far more than controversial – it could be counted on to make you the laughingstock of the community. And yet your motives would be pure. The idea is innovative and there is every possibility that it would reduce economic and social costs to the community. So why exactly are your fellow citizens waving their arms and screaming abuse at you?

The reasons are many, and mostly have to do with the part of us that feels rather than the part that thinks. But there is one overwhelming reason why that speech would probably end your hope of a career in public service.

You would be asking your fellow citizens for a drastic change of heart on a very touchy subject.

The Challenge of Change

More than two thousand five hundred years ago, Siddhārtha Gautama – better known as the Buddha – observed the curious fact that life consists of nothing but change, yet we fear and resist change with all our might and put our faith in the changeless. Horses and buggies get us around in one century, automobiles the next and solar-powered flying cars (we hope) the next. The traveling troubadour gives way to the vinyl record, the transistor radio, the Walkman, the iPod and the iTunes store. People are born, they mature in body and mind, they grow old and they die. By the time you finish reading this sentence, 50 million of the cells in your body will have died and been replaced, out of 30-40 trillion cells that answer to your name.[171]

Change has always been with us. We don't like it any better now than we did in the Buddha's day, or when his contemporary Heraclitus of Greece wrote that "No man ever steps in the same river twice, for it's not the same river and he's not the same man."

Amsterdam's Rainbow Foundation was trying neither to cure people of alcoholism nor punish them for it when it started paying street cleaners in beer. The Foundation was just helping them find a useful place in society for their own good and that of everyone around them. To accept the wisdom of this experiment, however, you may have to surrender deeply-held notions about what the wages of sin ought to be, who is worthy of our compassion, and for what purposes public money should be spent. Maybe you are willing to do so; maybe you are not. When it comes to this kind of change, most of us would check the "maybe not" box in a heartbeat.

The trouble is that our new century is challenging us with profound change at a pace never before imagined, driven by the information and communications technologies that have so drastically accelerated the global economy.

Two economists at the University of California at Berkley, Hal Varian and Peter Lyman, made an attempt several years ago to estimate the world's output of information. They measured the total production of all information channels in 2000 – paper, film, tape, digital media, TV, radio, you name it – and filtered out duplication: a newly recorded song was considered information but the copies of that song playing across radio or sold at retail were not.

Having put in all this work, they estimated that the world produced about 1.5 exabytes of information in 2000. An exabyte is one of those techie words we wish we didn't have to cope with but probably do. It means one billion gigabytes or 37,000 times the information stored by the US Library of Congress. It's a lot.

The team also produced an estimate for 2003. It was 3.5 exabytes. Also a very big number. More important, however, it represented a 66% rate of annual growth. That is amazing.

To understand just how amazing, let's say we give you a gift of 10 grains of rice today. Tomorrow, we increase the gift by 66%, giving you 17 grains of rice. The next day, we bump up the gift again by 66% and so on for a month. On the 30th day, you would be the proud owner of a pile of rice taking up about as much space and weighing as much as a midsize automobile. Just finding a place to park it would be hard.

This book has argued that everything we do involving information – and that covers most things we do economically, socially and culturally – is following the same curve. The number of mobile broadband subscriptions grew 40% from 2010 to 2011 worldwide, which has helped make Twitter and Facebook the opportunity and threat that they are for today's political leaders. [172]

This chapter is about how some very smart people leading cities and regions have tried to respond to this extraordinary and accelerating rate of change, and what we can learn from their successes and failures.

How to Stop Wasting Our Potential

In 1994, the City of Riverside, in the US state of California, elected Ronald Loveridge as its mayor. Mr. Loveridge was a political science professor at the University of California Riverside and had served on the City Council since 1979. After a few years as mayor, however, this long-time member of Riverside's political establishment decided that it was time for his community to embrace some serious change.

Not that there was anything so terribly wrong in this city of 300,000, located in a region known as the Inland Empire 60 miles east of Los Angeles. It was a fast-growing bedroom community with attractive housing costs for those willing to endure the long commute to the City of Angels. Its low costs and ample land had also made it a warehousing and distribution center, where more than 120 trains a day passed on their way from the Port of Los Angeles. And it had UC Riverside, where 48,000 students contributed to the housing and retail economy.

But the problems were also evident for those with eyes to see. Smog was a hot-button issue. So was the heavy traffic caused by the economy's reliance on commuting and on transport by train and truck. The two issues were closely connected: in southern California, the two principal sources of air pollution are tailpipe emissions from cars and diesel pollution from trucks, trains and ships.

Riverside was also a socially divided place, with 49% of its population Hispanic and 34% white. While more than 15% of residents attended or worked at UC Riverside, 10% were low-income, poorly-paid manual workers employed by distribution and agriculture. They had proved fertile recruiting ground for the gang culture that spilled inland from the coast.

Fast population growth driven by commuters was gradually outstripping the ability of city government to manage it, and the strain was showing in multiple areas. In the Nineties, the city outsourced its entire information technology department, which wound up delivering greater value to the outsourcer than to city government. A controversial 1998 shooting of a 19-year-old sleeping in her disabled car led California's attorney general to issue a consent decree requiring the city to reform its police department. Implementing the changes cost the city $7 million for training, education and equipment.[173]

As a university professor, Mayor Loveridge believed that one problem loomed larger than all the rest: his city was wasting the potential of its role as home of UC Riverside. With most of its economy effectively outsourced to the Los Angeles, the city offered too few opportunities to the university's graduating classes. When they left, they took their diplomas and brainpower with them.

California is known for its high-tech companies, and Riverside had a few: IO Software, Surado Solutions, Qmotions, Fata Hunter and Luminex. In 2004, the CEOs of those companies went to the Dean of the Bourns College of Engineering at UC Riverside and asked his help in forming a local network they wanted to call the Riverside Technology CEO Forum. They held meetings and shared best practices in an effort to help everybody's businesses to grow. It was the start of something – but only a start.

"Mayor Loveridge met this guy named John Tillquist, who was married to his chief of staff," explains Steve Reneker, whom Riverside would later hire as its chief information officer. "Tillquist was a successful technology entrepreneur who was semi-retired and teaching at UC Riverside. He and the mayor started having conversations, and the guy proposed to develop a report for Council that outlined strategic initiatives for Riverside, and to put his own time into getting stakeholders around the city to buy into it."

With the mayor's backing, Professor Tillquist reached out in 2004 to the new CEO Forum for help. This report was not intended to wind up in a desk drawer but to be a catalyst for change. So developing the report was much more than an act of analysis and writing; it was a rallying point for all those who thought they had better ideas for Riverside's future. The volunteer group that rallied around the flag called itself the High Technology Task Force.

"We had to figure out how to bring people to the table," says Mr. Loveridge. "We had a number of business leaders in the Chamber of Commerce and the CEO Forum. We had guys from Tech Coast Angels. John Tillquist became the principal author of the report, *A Blueprint for High Technology in Riverside.* When we went to Council, one council member said that it was the best report he had ever seen. It was clear, gave specific direction and went into detail about how collaboration would take place. So many reports like this are impenetrable, but John did a great job."

The report, which took eight months to produce, issued a bold challenge to the status quo. "Riverside's historical reliance on 'cheap dirt' real estate has spawned numerous warehousing and other land-intensive, low-technology businesses," it began, and went on:

> *Marketing emphasis on low utility rates has brought in a number of low-tech, high-usage manufacturing, production and low-wage services. However, with a sizable government employment base, the presence of four institutions of higher education and a growing population of increasingly educated and wealthy residents emigrating from the coastal communities, Riverside lays claim to a diverse economic base and growing metropolitan momentum. These factors, both positive and negative, place Riverside at an economic crossroads.*

The High Tech Task Force was in no doubt about which road the community should take. It recommended a major effort to promote local high-tech business development, introduce high-quality broadband, make the city a strategic user of IT and stimulate technology entrepreneurship.

The City Council was quick to accept the recommendations and Assistant City Manager Mike Peck was made responsible for implementing them in collaboration with the Task Force. "Once the report was presented," says Mr. Loveridge, "the Council asked for progress reports every 90 days. I pushed it as Mayor and Mike pushed it from city hall. The issue was to create energy and momentum."

A CIO Takes Charge

One recommendation in the report was for Riverside to regain control of its information technology. The city hired Steve Reneker as its new CIO and tasked him with rebuilding an IT department. Reneker had experience in the public-sector through IT management positions with Riverside County and one of southern California's water districts. He had also worked in IT for the banking industry and in business development for Dell, which gave him the ability to talk the language of both business and government.

Reneker renegotiated the city's IT outsourcing contract to a "cost plus" formula that saved more than $4 million. He ploughed the savings into refreshing the city's technology, building a fiber backbone to connect city facilities, and creating a network operations center. He also went shopping for a carrier that would build him a wireless broadband network across the city. It was during a short-lived period when carriers like Earthlink, AT&T and Sprint thought they could make money by building free Wi-Fi networks in US cities and selling online advertising on the networks to local businesses. Reneker signed a contract with AT&T to deploy a 1,600-node city-wide wireless network providing 1 Mbps broadband to residents and city departments, as well as a separate frequency band for public safety.

"The wireless network had some unexpected challenges," says Reneker. "Not because of lack of political support or the performance of the vendor. It came down to changing ordinances. To support the network, the Council passed ordinances that required building owners to eliminate 'leaky coax' – poorly shielded data cabling that puts out radio interference – and put money into in-building wireless repeaters for the public-safety frequencies. It wasn't a benefit for business – they had to pay for it – but it meant that first-responders had radio and cell communications inside large facilities. It took some effort but the benefit was clear and we got the support from business that we needed."

By 2010, AT&T exited the business and transferred ownership to the city – but the project had done its job. It proved the strong demand for broadband service in Riverside, and persuaded Verizon, Charter Cable and other carriers to begin deploying 20-50 Mbps service to homes and businesses. By 2014, as the wireless network was showing its age, the city began grappling with whether to invest in upgrading it or shut it down.[174]

Using the wireless network and its own fiber, the city installed cameras at intersections and railroad crossings, updated its traffic signals for remote control and created a traffic management center to manage the complex flow of traffic and trains. Average commute times through the city quickly fell by 30 percent.

Reneker's pride and joy was an award-winning project that used IT to tackle the problem of graffiti. Using a smartphone app, anyone from a city worker to a citizen can snap a photo of graffiti and submit it to the city, complete with time, date and location information. The image is put through pattern-recognition software that seeks to match it to the system's growing database of images. Because much of the city's graffiti consisted of the "tags" that gangs use to mark their territory, the system is pretty effective at matching a new piece of graffiti to the gang and artist. The system automatically alerts the City Attorney and provides background information for preparation of a criminal prosecution, while it generates a work order for removal of the graffiti.

Within a matter of years, successful prosecutions generated $200,000 in income from fines for the city, helping to pay for its cost while improving the image of the city in the eyes of citizens.

Image was a vital concern to Reneker. "We apply for a lot of awards," he says, "because it lets people know we want to be a high-tech community. We changed Riverside's motto to 'The City of Arts and Innovation' to tell people who we are. We innovated in services for residents, from a single 311 number for city services to mobile apps, so that people saw the positive results of change in their own lives."

So, while doing the things a smart CIO does, Reneker insisted on stepping far outside the IT box. With the Council's support, he took over a nonprofit organization founded by the city called Riverside Community Online. It was originally tasked with building a website, but Reneker renamed it Smart-Riverside and used it, in collaboration with the Task Force and CEO Forum, to drive the eight initiatives recommended in *A Blueprint for High Technology in Riverside*.

This is where the partnerships forged by the city with its business sector began to pay off. In most places, city government or a local university sets up a business incubator in hopes of fostering startups. In Riverside, it was the tech companies that lead the way. ISCA, which uses electronic technologies to solve pest problems, began offering office space and production facilities for startups in 2008. Bourns, a manufacturer of electronic components, established a second incubator in 2009, and Surado Solutions, maker of customer relationship management systems, included incubator space in its new Surado Corporate Center.

By 2011, when the Innovation Economy Corporation partnered with the city and UC Riverside to create the city's first dedicated incubator, it was betting on a model that had already proven its success. Completing the business-government-education circle, Riverside Community College created the Tritech Business Development Center, which went on to train 270 potential entrepreneurs and help 20 tech startups to get off the ground.

In 2012, Riverside was named ICF's Intelligent Community of the Year, and Steve Reneker – now the CIO of Los Angeles – credits collaboration for the win. "In putting the programs together, collaboration was the key – and if it wasn't for the Mayor driving it, we wouldn't be where we are today. We had a lot of different groups at work, but they weren't working together. When Mayor Loveridge brought together educators, administrators, businesspeople and emergency workers to see that their problems and opportunities were connected, the light finally went on."

Transformation Without Trauma

In 2006, the city of Birmingham in the English Midlands launched a 10-year project to transform how its government did business. Such re-engineering projects have a dismal success rate, but Birmingham had good reasons to try.

Like many old industrial cities and much of the UK's Midlands, Birmingham had been enormously successful in the 19th and early 20th Centuries. But deindustrialization in the 1980s brought its economy to the brink of collapse. Massive urban redevelopment since then has reshaped the city's outward face but the scars of that trauma lingered in people's lives and in how the city was governed.

As the UK's second most populous city, Birmingham's government was responsible for maintaining 68,000 homes, 2,500 kilometers of roads, 400 schools and 41 libraries.[175] Yet financial reporting was poor, which gave City Council very limited visibility into city finances, and led to on-time payment of only two-thirds of the city's bills. Surveys showed that citizens and businesses had a low opinion of city government because it was hard to reach someone to address their problems and even harder to get follow-through. A national inspection program, which rated municipalities on a four-star scale, gave Birmingham just one star and went on to suggest that improvement was unlikely.[176]

To tackle the challenge, the Council hired Glyn Evans as Director of Business Solutions & IT in November 2003. He inherited a department of 500 people with an annual budget of about $80 million to support 20,000 desktops across 1,000 locations. Maintaining the status quo, however, was neither his intention nor his mandate. Like Reneker in Riverside, he founded a new organization – this one called Digital Birmingham – as a partnership of public, private and volunteer sector organizations. Its goal was to focus far beyond information technology to its application in supporting economic, social and environmental regeneration.

Digital Birmingham launched a lot of projects, some with local funding, others with national or European Commission money. It partnered with a local charity, St. Basil's, to create a Virtual Rucksack, which gave homeless people in Birmingham a safe place to store and access personal information such as national insurance numbers, bank details and work and address histories.[177] It launched an annual Hello

Digital Week, whose first year attracted over 1,000 delegates from 22 European cities and showcased the region's technology achievements. The Go ON Birmingham campaign, launched in 2012, aimed to create 2,000 digital champions among citizens, who help their friends, relatives and colleagues get online and improve their digital skills. Digital Birmingham proposed investing US$16 million to bring ultrafast broadband to a new Enterprise Zone in the city center and the creation of Digital Districts as models of mixed-use development focused on broadband.[178]

These projects were down payments on change. Public-private programs like these will, if maintained and adapted to changing conditions, produce lasting transformation – but generally at a slow pace. "If you tell the public what you're going to do," said Evans, "they're not very interested unless it impacts them, such as deciding to build a prison at the end of their street. So, when we started, we talked about the need to improve services for the public and save money while we were at it. What we did with various levels of success was to involve particular groups in the design process. We would get direct input into what we're doing and then feed the results out to the public."

Having seen many projects launched, Evans turned his attention to creating faster change where the City Council had the greatest traction: its own operations. By 2006, Evans had developed and won Council approval of plan requiring investment of $988 million to achieve $3.3 billion in benefits, of which $2.4 billion would be in the form of cash savings.

To manage the project, the city entered a public-private partnership, in which the city owned one-third, with Capita, a UK outsourcing firm. The new company was called Service Birmingham and was granted an exclusive contract for delivery and support of ICT as key building blocks of the transformation program. At the same time, Glyn Evans got a new title better fitting his real responsibility: Corporate Director of Business Change.

The Burning Platform

The plan called for the city to borrow the necessary funds. For better or worse, taking on debt turned what could have been a slow, behind-the-scenes evolution into a high-wire act played out in public, with a great deal of political fallout in the case of failure.

"In change management," Evans said, "the literature says that you have to 'identify the burning platform.' The problem is that there is rarely a burning platform in the public sector." A $988 million bet on the future filled the gap nicely.

But was not enough that Evans felt the heat. "What is essential," he said, "is putting in the time to win around the top political and administrative leaders, so that they feel they own it, are accountable for it and have skin in the game. In previous positions, my key mistake was to take a report to the leaders and get them to agree – but when things went wrong, they had no ownership and didn't defend it."

Creating the right structure helped. "One of the things we got right," Evans added, "was to truly engage political leaders in the process. The transformation program was divided into 9 sub-programs. For each one, we found a political leader and an administrative leader to head it. The rules said that without both of them in attendance, no meeting would have a quorum for decision. We also came up with a flow of short, readable reports that kept them informed and, most important of all, let them know when something was falling behind."

No process could have succeeded, however, without public leadership. "We got lucky in our Council. Our current deputy leader, Sir Paul Tisley, became our chief political sponsor. After spending 30 years in opposition, when he became deputy leader, he wanted things to happen and wanted them done well."

But not even Paul Tisley could make the seas part. "We have 120 councilors, of whom ten are cabinet members, ten or twelve are on important committees and everybody else is a backbencher. It is very hard to engage and inform the backbenchers. If you call a workshop, they have no issue about not showing up, but when they see an outcome they don't like, they are hammering on your door. We have never been able to crack that."

In 2011, at the midpoint of the transformation process, the city presented its results in a case study.[179] The overarching goals of the program were to improve service delivery to citizens and businesses, achieve greater efficiency and lower costs, and improve job satisfaction for the city's 50,000 employees.

The investments in ICT produced a system that offered Council up-to-date financial information on a continuing basis, compared with the three months previously required for reporting. The percentage of invoices paid within 30 days rose from one-third in 2006 to 96%. A welter of more than 400 contact telephone numbers was replaced with a single number giving access to a network of customer service centers, where 80% of the two million calls received per year were answered in 19 seconds or less and customer satisfaction ratings topped 95%. Online, a modernized web site has led 13,000 citizens and businesses to open individual accounts, from which they can make requests and track progress.

The city also consolidated 55 administrative buildings into just eight new sites, following a 30% reduction in back office staff. An Amazon-style procurement Internet of Things site for employees began generating annual savings of $115 million. Two-thirds of housing benefit claims were completed on the phone without need for a face-to-face appointment, and benefits claims were being paid 50% faster than through the old manual methods.

Midway through the process, Birmingham had achieved $407 million in benefits – 13% of the end goal – of which a total of $157 million (6% of the annual goal) were in annual recurring savings. Best of all, on the cash borrowed for the project, the Council had made it into the black with net savings of $25 million in the fiscal year.

So, the headlines were good, or should have been. "There's a part of Birmingham's culture that focuses on the negative." Glyn Evans said. "We suffer from that. We have had our bits of bad news and my approach has been to make it as transparent as possible. It's not sensible just to announce the bad news: you have to explain what you're doing about it. We have a very skeptical press. Bad news is on the front page, good news on page 17."

Still, despite the occasional slip, the project has made measurable progress toward its goals while being a good steward of the people's money. "We've never had a catastrophe," Evans added, who left Birmingham City Council for the private sector in 2012. "I don't think a change program can survive a catastrophe. Catastrophes put down deep roots. We have had teething problems with people and processes. It can be just 5% of the total but it can create a sense of failure. You need to proactively manage expectations, let people know that glitches will happen and that they can be managed."

Birmingham's transformation initiative was well-timed. In 2010, in response to the continuing recession in the wake of the financial crisis, Britain's government began a series of severe budget cuts that rippled through the finances of municipalities. (British cities receive most of their funding from the national government.) Having tackled service improvements and cost cuts beginning four years earlier, Birmingham had a platform in place to handle the stresses and integrate them into its continuing effort at regeneration.

Home of the Corn Palace

Thousands of miles to the west of Birmingham lies the city of Mitchell, South Dakota, USA, which we cited as a model rural community. While Birmingham is home to slightly more than one million people, Mitchell counts 15,000 citizens. Given its location, it should come as no surprise that the dominant building downtown is the Corn Palace, a tribute to Mitchell's contribution to the $167 billion worth of annual corn production in the United States.[180]

For Mitchell and many other rural communities in the US, agriculture is a blessing and a curse. It is subject to economic cycles as prices rise and fall though government subsidy schemes ensure long-term stability. The trouble is that agriculture just doesn't provide very many jobs because automation from farm to store has been so effective.

"As far back as the 1950s," said Bryan Hisel, Executive Director of the Mitchell Area Development Corporation, "it was becoming obvious to business leaders that the agricultural economy was not going to require a lot of population. Jobs were going to have to come from somewhere else."

The success of agriculture did breed jobs in other sectors, mostly retail, food service and accommodations. But it was not employment that could sustain a prosperous middle class.

So, like most places, Mitchell began chasing smokestacks – companies that would locate a facility within the city limits.

"We had some success," said Hisel. "3M was here, and that deal led to a location decision by Toshiba. But a lot of it didn't last. We recruited a floppy disk manufacturer and a maker of microwavable food products. Neither of them stayed with us. Slowly, over too much time, we began to see that the best companies in town were those that were started here and grew here. We still do business attraction, but we are much more selective and much more honest. What skills are the companies looking for? How much will the jobs pay? If a company needs hundreds of employees, they are not going to find them here, waiting to put in a job application, because the rural workforce is smaller. One thing we do not do much anymore is writing big checks to out-of-state employers to persuade them to locate here."

That is true, in no small part, because Mitchell found a better way. The city came to it, however, by a winding road.

The People Say 'No'
The history of telecommunications in rural areas is largely one of being bypassed. Urban areas, where subscribers live cheek by jowl, take much less investment per subscriber to generate revenue for a communications carrier, compared with rural areas where subscribers may live many miles or kilometers apart. So, they vote their preferences with their investment dollars or euros, yen or pesos.

In the United States, rural areas have responded by creating cooperative telephone companies owned by their subscribers, dating back to Joseph Gliddens' invention of barbed wire. They gave rise to thousands of more formal businesses, but their roots ensured that community service remained important to their missions.

In 1989, a group of 17 rural telephone cooperatives joined forces to create the South Dakota Network, or SDN Communications as it is now known. SDN began building a high-capacity network linking anchor institutions – government, schools, libraries, and hospitals – throughout South Dakota, as both a profitable business and a public service.[181]

"Without the South Dakota Network," says Roger Musick, CEO of Innovative Systems in Mitchell and one of the champions for change in the business community, "Mitchell could not have taken the next step. People began experiencing the Broadband Economy in their lives. It brought us electronic healthcare by connecting our hospital to a network of 130 others for intensive care, pharmacy and emergency room services. It literally made the internet viable for hundreds of places like Mitchell."

By the time that the US Government launched its broadband stimulus program in 2009, SDN had grown to 27 member companies that connected 220 anchor institutions across the state through a 1,850-mile fiber-optic network. The company won a stimulus grant that funded construction of an additional 140 miles of backbone network and 219 miles of middle mile to reach another 300 institutions and boost speeds to 10 Mbps.[182]

By that time, however, Mitchell's leaders had already put the telecommunications future of their city to public vote – and lost. "We attempted in 1997 to create a municipally-owned broadband network to deliver the triple play of telephone, internet and television," said Bryan Hisel. "The president of the communications program at Mitchell Technical Institute came up with the idea. Our business community was heavily in favor. We put together the business plan and proposed to the public that we create a new public utility and issue bonds to pay for development."

"The public looked at the tax bill and said 'no,'" said Mitchell Mayor Ken Tracy, who first joined City Council in 2000 after the failed vote. "As a citizen at that time, I have to say it was complicated and not well understood. Our voting population, when they don't understand something, tends to vote against it. We also faced incumbents who financed a vigorous campaign against the proposal, devoting far more resources than the city."

The failed vote looked like the end of the story at the time, but it turned out to be the beginning of a new chapter. It is a surprising thing, but when a municipality demonstrates real hell-for-leather resolve to bring in broadband, it has a way of changing the investment equation for the private sector. The cable television company found that – while an old coaxial cable network had seemed appropriate for the Mitchell market before the vote – that same market now justified an investment in optical fiber. The incumbent telephone company put Mitchell on its list of communities to receive a wireless upgrade to 4G service.

The Mitchell Technical Institute (MTI), whose vision had sparked the vote, built a Technology Center to serve students and the community. It attracted the attention of competitive local exchange carriers in the region as a place to house their equipment. MTI applied for and won a grant to build a Network Operations Center (NOC) in the Technology Center as a service platform for private-sector carriers. It was not long before a competitive local exchange carrier (CLEC) won a low-interest loan from the Rural Utilities Service of the US Department of Agriculture and began constructing an end-to-end fiber-to-the-home network.

On this foundation, institutions, business and government have collaborated intensively to drive economic development. The school district launched a 1:1 laptop program for secondary school students and a pilot program in "mass customization" of learning, which aims to give students education appropriate to their individual abilities. It opened a Career and Technical Education Center in partnership with MTI and Mitchell's Dakota Wesleyan University to equip students with the skills in greatest local demand: agriculture, health care, energy, construction and communications.

Two hospitals merged to create Mitchell's largest employer, which draws staff from the graduates leaving Dakota Wesleyan and MTI each year. The broadband buildouts have led to the formation of three new engineering, consulting and software companies that employ more than 500 professionals and technicians. With new tech-centered office properties rising and hundreds of citizen volunteers engaged in promoting its vision, Mitchell has constructed a whole new economy on top of its agricultural one, which both supports the success of agriculture and offers opportunities far beyond it.

Now wait a minute, you may be thinking. In the late Nineties, the people are voting 'no' and a decade later, broadband and information technology are a significant economic force in Mitchell. How did it happen?

"There are not too many problems," said Bryan Hisel, "that can't be solved over a cup of coffee – if I can just manage to drink enough cups of coffee in a day."

"We have a core group of people who serve on boards, from MTI to the university to the Chamber of Commerce and the hospital," added Roger Musick. "It's a significant group made up of the same people with similar goals. In one classic example, the university started an entrepreneurship program and the guy tapped to lead it was Bryan Hisel."

Mayor Tracy agrees. "We have recognized within our community those individuals who assume leadership in pushing forward programs like this – but also more familiar things like a new swimming pool or soccer field. There is a core of people who are seen as strong community leaders. As Mayor, through the City Council, I call them to serve and they answer the call. It has been very beneficial."

There are more formal processes as well, which add rigor and accountability to the personal networks. "Back in the Nineties," said Hisel, "we launched a Vision 2000 process that brought together a couple hundred people to figure out where our community should be going. We did it again with a Focus 2020 project that set goals for quality of life, education and the economy. Day-to-day, the connections in a community of 15,000 are pretty easy – there are only so many people who are interested enough to be a leader. Roger Musick is one of them: I sometimes forget that, with his service on the university board and economic development board, he also has a company to run."

That collaborative spirit and network of commitments among leaders laid the foundation, but they were not sufficient to the day. "One thing we learned from that failed vote," said Mayor Tracy, "is that education is the key to success. We need to be open and honest with voters. We need to work hard to gain their support. Bryan's group has done a study to determine what factors make a difference to Mitchell's economy. We published that and made the results widely known. Another study analyzed our current shortage in rental housing – the product of being successful at creating jobs – and led to construction of 200 new apartments."

Sir Winston Churchill may have observed that "the best argument against democracy is a five-minute conversation with the average voter." But in Riverside, Birmingham and Mitchell, the deep involvement of voters was the engine that ultimately powered success, even if the message delivered by those voters was sometimes negative. "We have waxed and waned in terms of political support," Bryan Hisel said. "If people have good jobs and their homes are appreciating in value, if we have enough tax revenue to care for the community, that creates all the political support needed."

Efforts to create change cannot always succeed. America's Abraham Lincoln once noted that "elections belong to the people. It's their decision. If they decide to turn their back on the fire and burn their behinds, then they will just have to sit on their blisters."

It is when the fire is hottest that the informal leadership network of a community can be most important. Leaders in business and the nonprofit worlds have networks of their own – sectors of the community where their opinions count most – and if they are committed to the vision and the process, they can help the elected and administrative leadership survive setbacks and live to fight another day.

The paramount factor is trust. The leaders of Intelligent Communities are skilled at creating trust built on transparency, clarity and honesty in acknowledging successes and failures. When citizens trust their leaders and share their vision, there is very little that can stop a community from achieving its aims.

Brain Gain

CHAPTER TWELVE
Getting into Heaven

Despite being an atheist, I often imagine Saint Peter at the gates of heaven asking me to justify my life. Saying "I helped eliminate the need for skill in the world" is not a great recommendation for admittance.[183]

John Goodman, a software developer who builds automation systems, wrote those words in a letter to the editor of *The Atlantic* in early 2014. He was responding to an article about our accelerating ability to automate business processes, not just the routine physical ones, but increasingly those requiring analytic ability and a degree of judgment. The impact, of course, is to replace human workers with software, which never gets tired or hungry, sick or addicted, and has no pesky dependents to be fed, clothed and sheltered. These expert systems are built by collecting, analyzing and digitizing human knowledge, but their effect is to make humans unnecessary to yet another task.

This is how far we have come in the twenty years since Netscape introduced the first commercial Internet of Things browser and kicked the ICT revolution into overdrive. The ride has been a wild one for workers in rich, middle-income and emerging economies, and for the communities where they live.

Slowly, through sometimes painful experience, communities have learned that brain gain is not just an issue of importance – it is the whole ballgame. Developing a skilled workforce, and having a plentiful supply of jobs (and wages) that match their skills, is the foundation of prosperity. But if the pace of job destruction and creation is vastly speeding up, will it exceed the pace at which human beings can adapt? If the next wave of digital innovation is going to replace skilled people with skillful software at an ever-greater rate, where will tomorrow's prosperity come from?

Lots of digital and physical ink have been spilled trying to answer that question. Putting speculation and fear to one side, however, there are a few things we actually *know,* as well as some reasoned guesses we can make about the future of the brain gain/drain balance, and what communities can do to get on the right side of it.

The Near-Zero Effect

One of the things we know is that digital technologies have an impact unlike any other technology advance in history. It was first demonstrated in 1999 by Napster, an online service that let millions of people share music without paying the artists, distributors or rights holders. Though Napster was eventually shut down for – well, for basically stealing other people's stuff – it pioneered a new way of consuming music, and the recording industry and artists took a huge hit from which they have yet to recover.

Before Napster, recording artists and their studios had long allowed their music to be played on the radio for pennies because it stimulated sales of millions of records. Today's artists and studios have had to adapt to a world in which they are largely giving the music away in order to generate income from concerts and product sales.

The same disruption has slammed the newspaper business. In the US, annual newspaper print ad revenue was about $65 billion in 2000. Twelve years later, in 2012, it had shrunk to only $19 billion, because classified advertising went almost entirely to the Internet of Things.[184] Television broadcasting and the movie industry find themselves under threat as well from upstarts like Netflix, and digital giants like Microsoft now offer their software through a low-cost monthly subscription rather than costly purchases.

All of this has happened because of the positively weird economics of digital in a world of widespread broadband. It still costs a lot to produce a musical recording, a news story or a TV show. But once the thing is produced, the cost of producing the next digital copy is close to zero. Once I possess a digital copy, I can reproduce and distribute it at a cost of near-zero to as many other people as I happen to know.

Digital, then, tends to drive the cost and price of everything toward zero. You may have heard that phrase before – but have you stopped to think about what it really means?

Countless innovations over centuries have made big improvements in cost and efficiency. One of the least heralded but most profound was the lowly cargo container. In 1956, the first prototype container ship set sale, carrying a set of standard containers sized to fit on a truck trailer instead of the usual mass of loose cargo. The container was the brainchild of American trucking magnate Malcolm McLean. When he tallied up the costs of that first voyage, he found that they came to just $1.16 per metric ton to load, compared with $5.83 per metric ton for loose cargo. In 1965, longshoremen could load only 1.7 metric tons per hour onto a ship; just five years later, as ports adopted the container, a loading crew could put 30 metric tons on board in the same time.[185]

Impressive, right? But it's not zero. There is still additional cost attached to each additional bit of cargo. The tendency of digital to drive costs toward zero poses challenges to whole industries that will be reverberating through our lives for decades.

Decades, because we are still in the early stages of this thing. The massively open online course or MOOC, discussed in a previous chapter, has the same economics as a song on iTunes: make it once and distribute an unlimited number of times at near-zero cost.

The Near-Zero Effect of digital is even beginning to leak into the physical world. The introduction of 3D printing brings Near-Zero economics to manufacturing. The printer is a sophisticated machine but, like a computer, it is a generalist that can print many different things – which is a complete departure from the traditional process. The printer's contribution to the value of the finished product is small compared with assembly-line equipment; the real value lies in the digital model and the instructions that drive the printer.

"3D printers open up the possibility of more distributed production networks and radical customization," says an article from McKinsey & Co, which forecasts that printer sales will double to US$4 billion from 2013 to 2015. "It's easy to imagine the emergence of service businesses – the equivalent of copy or print shops – that would manufacture items based on design specifications provided by customers. Crowdsourcing networks for new product ideas could one day complement traditional R&D activities."[186]

And if you really want your mind blown, innovators are working on ways to use 3D printing technology to build components for you. "The promise of 3D bioprinting is even larger: to create human tissues – layer by layer – for research, drug development and testing, and ultimately as replacement organs," reported *The Economist* in March 2014. "Bioprinted organs could be made from patients' own cells and thus would not be rejected by their immune systems. They could also be manufactured on demand." [187]

Or take energy. It costs a lot to build a windmill or banks of solar panels. But once they are in place, the cost of capturing each unit of energy is low, because the fuel is free. It is a fundamentally different model from fossil-fuel power generation. Economic and social critic Jeremy Rifkin has combined this fact with a vision of the Internet of Things – the 50 billion sensors that are expected to connect to the Internet of Things by 2020 – to forecast a change in how we consume electricity:

> *People can connect to the network and use big data, analytics and algorithms to accelerate efficiency and lower the marginal cost of producing and sharing a wide range of products and services to near zero...For example, 37 million buildings in the United States have been equipped with meters and sensors connected to the Internet of Things, providing real-time information on the usage and changing price of electricity on the grid. This will eventually allow households and businesses that are generating and storing green electricity onsite from their solar and wind installations to program software to take them off the grid when prices spike so they can power their facilities with their own green electricity and share surplus with neighbors at near zero marginal cost.*[188]

Mr. Rifkin does not address how all those nimble facilities, taking themselves off the grid whenever prices rise, will affect the electric utilities. The early signs, however, are not encouraging.

Germany is a world leader in generating electricity from wind and solar. On a June day in 2013, one with bright sunshine and reasonable offshore breezes, the country generated a record 60% of its electricity from renewables. Great news, right? Not for the utilities that must, under regulations, buy that power at relatively high cost and cut back their own, much cheaper generating capacity. Not great news for the environment, either, because utilities have to maintain generating capacity that they can quickly bring online as day turns to night and breeze turns to calm. As noted by *The Economist*:

> *Across Europe a strange consequence of subsidized renewables is that some governments now want to pay power companies to maintain the capacity to produce electricity from fossil fuels to ensure that backup power is available. More perversely, Europe is burning more heavily polluting coal at the expense of cleaner and more flexible gas, because coal is cheap, the gas market is far from liquid and the carbon-emissions systems is broken.* [189]

In a market economy, we depend on changing prices to balance supply and demand. Higher demand tends to raise prices while also encouraging an increase in supply, which tends to drive prices back down. But in a Near-Zero world, those familiar market forces may not operate as expected. Whole industries will be reshaped as a result, with effects on employment that are hard to predict. Mr. Rifkin sees plenty of upside:

> *The answer lies in civil society, which consists of non-profit organizations that attend to the things in life we make and share as a community...New employment opportunities lie in the collaborative commons in fields that tend to be nonprofit and strengthen social infra-structure – education, health care, aiding the poor, environmental restoration, child care and care for the*

*elderly...We are entering a world partly beyond markets,
where we are learning how to live together in an
increasingly interdependent, collaborative, global
commons.*[190]

Let us hope that his vision is true. It sounds like a world
that most of us would like to live in. But odds are, the road to
that future will contain more than a few potholes.

Bad News from the Gig Economy

Another thing we know is that the Near-Zero Effect is not just
a challenge for business. In March 2014, Sarah Kessler
reported in an article in *Fast Company* magazine on her
attempt to make a living in what she called the Gig Economy.
She registered for such Internet of Things-based hire-an-
assistant services as Fiverr, Postmates, Task Rabbit and
Amazon's Mechanical Turk, and bid on assignments. While
doing a Mechanical Turk project – labeling slides for a
Microsoft researcher – she had an epiphany:

> *On my way to completing 61 slideshows, I begin to resent
> Larry Zitnick, the Microsoft researcher who posted this
> maddening task. When I call him, he's actually quite
> nice. Zitnick explains that my slideshow labels are
> helping to train a computer to recognize images. "In the
> early 200s, our datasets generally had hundreds or
> maybe a few thousand images in them," he says. "And
> now we have datasets with millions of images in them.
> It's because of Mechanical Turk."*
>
> *Labeling slideshows suddenly feels very important.
> But it still doesn't pay. I make $1.94 an hour. Research
> suggests most people, like me, aren't making substantial
> income off their Mechanical Turk work. Only 8% of
> workers surveyed by researchers at the University of*

California, Irvine, said that Mechanical Turk income always helped them meet their basic needs.[191]

Services like these will hardly be the whole of the future economy – but they will definitely play their part. OnForce, another cloud-based service for matching freelancers to assignments, claims that "more than two million task assignments have been completed through OnForce's platform, and 5,000 enterprises including Apple, Comcast/Xfinity, AT&T and Xerox have used OnForce to engage, manage and pay independent contractors."[192] What it does not claim is that the power of the cloud, in this case, is helping to drive the price of such freelance services toward zero by creating a vast open marketplace for them.

Information and communications technology is on the verge of vastly expanding the range of jobs that we can trust machines to do instead of people. Google has made headlines for pioneering self-driving cars that substitute cameras, sensors and software for the skills of a driver. As of August 2012, a set of test cars driving around California had completed 300,000 miles of driving without accident.[193] In April 2014, Google announced that it had analyzed driving data from the US Centers for Disease Control and discovered that its robotic cars were a lot safer than ones with a human behind the wheel.[194] Numerous legal and insurance issues remain to be worked out before driverless cars hit the road without a human inside to backstop the system – but it requires little imagination to project a future where long-haul trucks, delivery vehicles, taxis and finally the individual passenger car will be driven principally by machines.

In 2012, 3.2 million Americans made their living as drivers of heavy trucks, taxis, limos and delivery vans.[195] One has to wonder how bright a future that particular category of employment has.

Drivers on land are not the only ones facing peril from ICT. The maritime industry is looking seriously at the idea of remote-controlled cargo ships setting sail without a crew. Ships are increasingly controlled by electronics anyway, their bridges filled with computer monitors and joysticks instead of the traditional engine telegraph and ship's wheel. If we are able to fly pilotless aircraft by remote control, how much easier would it be to control a slower-moving ship?

Most accidents at sea are the result of human error, so sensors and computer systems should make shipping safer. It will definitely make it cheaper; it is increasingly difficult and expensive today to sign crews for long voyages. Compare that with a future in which crews are put aboard just for entering and leaving port, while onshore control rooms will manage the rest of the voyage. Rolls Royce, which makes ship engines, estimates that a team of ten land-based captains could manage 100 ships at sea. No one expects cruise ship passengers to accept the idea of remote-controlled liners but the potential for cargo vessels is vast.[196]

Industrial robots were the villains (to workers) of the last great wave of industrial automation in the Eighties and Nineties. The threat to factory workers has not gone away. Investments in industrial robots have grown 50% since 2008, even in emerging nations like China, while they have gained in capability. Today's robots can perform intricate and demanding tasks like picking up small electronic parts and picking and packing products. Equipped with better sensors and smarter interfaces, they can work safely side by side with human beings and be managed by factory floor workers rather than programmers.

These advances are not good news for low-skilled factory employment. The McKinsey Global Institute projects that 15-25% more of the tasks of industrial workers in developed nations, and 5-15% more of those in developing countries, could be automated by 2025.[197]

Most importantly, they are networked – to each other, to factory management systems, and to the world. They are part of an emerging future in which manufacturers will gain unprecedented understanding and control of their operations. According to McKinsey:

> *They'll be able to run virtual operations "war rooms" on their phones. They'll have opportunities to solve plant-floor optimization problems as intelligent machines interface with each other and with people on the line...Manufacturers will pursue the buying and selling of previously underutilized production lines "by the hour" and will rely on dynamic databases to determine what every part should cost.*
>
> *GE already has a 400-person industrial internet software team and its employees use iPads to run an advanced battery factory. Amazon.com is employing growing numbers of smart warehouse robots...Alcoa has compressed prototyping time and costs and an auto supplier recently slashed an eight-month prototyping process to one week.[198]*

Manufacturing is not the only area where the march of the machines will be transformative. Gartner Group, a technology observatory, sees three major trends taking shape. Technology is going to be used to augment human abilities, as when people use wearable devices like Google Glass to do their jobs better. Machines and people are also going to work in collaboration – such as a mobile robot working with a warehouse employee to move boxes. And machines are going to take over jobs once reserved for human beings, as sophisticated voice recognition systems are already doing in telephone customer service. [199]

"Machines are becoming better at understanding humans and the environment," says Hung LeHong, a research vice president at Gartner, "for example, recognizing the emotion in a person's voice – and humans are becoming better at understanding machines – for example, through the Internet of Things. At the same time, humans and machines are getting smarter by working together."[200]

The Computer Will See You Now

Not even the most highly skilled jobs are immune. Doctors diagnose illness based on the knowledge in their heads – but the volume of medical information, already immense, grows at a pace no human can absorb. IBM's Watson computer can, however, based on continuously updated files of clinical information. In pilot projects, it is serving as a research assistant for doctors.

Reviewing symptoms inputted by the medical team, Watson matches them against its enormous database of possible diseases and offers alternatives for the doctor's consideration. For each diagnosis, Watson provides a confidence score, which allows the physician to judge the value of its advice. By backstopping the judgment of the doctor, Watson may help the human-machine team make the best-informed judgment.[201]

When a moderately powerful earthquake rattled the city of Los Angeles early on a March morning in 2014, the first news story was posted online just three minutes later. It was written by a computer program called Quakebot. Whenever an alert comes in from the US Geological Survey about an earthquake above a certain severity, Quakebot extracts the relevant data and plugs it into a pre-written template, which goes into the content management system of *The Los Angeles Times* for review by a human editor.[202]

A few days later, Kristian Hammond, a professor of computer science at Northwestern Engineering's McCormick School of Engineering, made a prediction that 90% of news stories would be written by computers by the year 2030. Dr. Hammond may be biased on the topic, though he is putting his money where his mouth is: he co-founded Narrative Science, which has developed software to fuse statistics with "journalistic clichés" to write simple news stories.[203]

In the first decade of the 21st Century, economists found themselves facing a puzzle. Throughout most of the previous century, the shares of national income going to labor (people) and to capital (owners and investors) were considered constant. When the economy expanded, labor and capital shared in the bounty; when the economy contracted, both felt the pain. That's what the numbers showed and that, economists believed, was how it would always be.

But the Organization for Economic Cooperation and Development (OECD), a club of mostly rich nations, has estimated that labor's share of national income fell from 66% in the early 1990s to just 62% in the 2000s. That means that productivity gains – the source of all economic growth – are less likely to translate into broad increases in pay. Instead, the owners of capital are getting a bigger share. So are the top earners, not because their salaries are so high but because they receive a big share of their income from – you guessed it – return on capital. The share of income earned by the top 1% of workers has increased since the 1900s even as labor's overall share has fallen.[204]

It is clear that something big is going on, something with bad consequences for most workers. This being economics, there are no sure answers – but the OECD did not hesitate to provide its own explanation. It believes the most probable cause of rising inequality is the very technology investment that is creating our whizz-bang future. It estimates technology to account for about 80% of the drop in labor's share of income, because technology's ability to reduce costs and increase efficiency makes it so attractive to continue swapping software and hardware for labor.

Them or Us?

So, is this what the future will come down to? Them versus us – machines versus people – and may the best entity win?

We must hope not.

If it really is a matter of robots taking our jobs – of every gain in productivity-enhancing technology crushing existing employment and creating none but those dreaded burger-flipping jobs – then it's no contest. We know how the story ends. In America, we learned to sing about it in elementary school: the story of John Henry, who went toe-to-toe with a steam engine and won but at the cost of his life, for he laid down his hammer and he died, Lord, Lord, he laid down his hammer and he died.

John Henry is a good touchstone on the subject, for it reminds us of the third thing that we really know.

The introduction of steam power in factories and transportation did not sharply reduce employment. Quite the reverse. From 1850 to 1870 – the Age of Steam, as it is known – US employment in some of the industries most affected by steam power – cotton textile weaving, iron and steel manufacturing and railways – *grew* by 32%, and the percentage of total manufacturing employment in all factories jumped from 44% to 72%.[205] The massive spread of steam power is estimated to have boosted the productivity of workers by more than 4% per year, which does not sound like much but is in fact huge. And that productivity increase seems to have *created* jobs, not destroyed them. [206]

The notion of technology change being the great destroyer of human labor is intuitively and emotionally obvious. It just does not happen to be right.

We believe it because we see the signs: the advent of steam drills did indeed put hammer-wielding navvies out of work, because the steam drill could do so much more in so much less time. The automatic teller machine did throw a lot of bank tellers out of work, just as automated call management systems reduced demand for receptions and speech recognition means we need fewer operators in our call centers. We see these things and reach the obvious conclusion. But we are wrong because we are missing part of the picture. As Ben Miller and Robert D. Atkinson succinctly put it in a September 2013 report:

> *The savings from new productivity gains must flow back to the economy in...lower prices, higher wages for the remaining employees or higher profits. It's important to recognize that productivity increases produce savings, even if firms have to buy machines or software to generate them. Why else would firms seek higher productivity? And these savings are not stuffed under the proverbial mattress[207].*

In short, when companies save money through productivity-enhancing technology, the money does not just disappear into thin air or the pockets of greedy capitalists. It gets spent. It flows back into the economy, generating new demand, whether for the same goods and services or new ones. That demand generates more production, which in turn creates demand for people to work. The hard part is that this demand for labor is often in completely different fields, so people do get thrown out of work, with all of the debilitating impact on lives and communities.

In 2005, the top 10 sectors for job growth in the United States included information services, healthcare, management, public relations, libraries, passenger transportation and legal services. Just eight years later, only two of those were still on the list: information services and healthcare. The rest were not. Libraries a growth business? Surely you jest. [208]

Productivity is Labor's Friend

Labor may win a lower proportion of total income in some decades and a bit more in others. In 2014, French economist Thomas Piketty published *Capital in the 21st Century*, which went on to become a highly unlikely best-seller. Based on centuries of statistics, it argued that the normal trend of capitalism is for the income from capital investments to grow much faster than the economy as a whole. In the second decade of the new century, for example, returns on capital in the US were 4 to 5 percent while the overall economy grew only 1.5 percent.

Labor's income, however, tends to grow no faster than the overall economy. Over time, according to Professor Piketty, this inevitably leads to capital grabbing more and more of the returns. We did not notice in the postwar years because two world wars destroyed so much capital investment that it took decades for the historical trends to reassert themselves. The postwar years were also a period of fast economic and population growth, and these tend to reduce inequality. Periods of slow growth, like those of the years beginning in 2010, have the opposite effect.[209]

We should certainly care about the relative distribution of gains and losses in the economy, and different nations will have different answers to the problem. But demonizing technology progress as a job-killing monster is not just wrong-headed. It is positively harmful. For what we really need is not less productivity but more. Higher productivity, ironically, is the only way for us all to prosper.

Higher productivity means cheaper goods and services. Cheaper goods and services mean that consumers can afford to buy more of them, and more consumer demand means more people are needed to produce the stuff to meet the demand. Those people get paid and their spending adds to the momentum of the economy.

In 2011, the McKinsey Global Institute examined annual employment and productivity change in the United States from the Depression year of 1929 through 2009. They found that gains in productivity are correlated with *increases* – not decreases – in subsequent employment. Counter-intuitive, right? In looking at 76 five-year slices of the data, only 8% of them featured both increasing productivity and declining employment. A snapshot of 2000-2007 shows an average annual gain of 2.7% in productivity and an average unemployment rate of only 2.7%. Compare that with 2008-2012, when productivity gains declined to below 2% while average unemployment leaped to nearly 8%.[210]

We have indulged ourselves in using American examples for much of this discussion because the US does a great job of capturing such data across its immense population, which shares a common language and set of laws. And despite the nation's political turmoil and the great economic advances of other countries, a high proportion of the world's technology future continues to be invented in America. It may be manufactured somewhere else, and some of its best ideas may find a better home in distant lands, but where America's technology disrupters go, the rest of the world continues to follow, at least for now.

Leaning into the Light

So, we can look forward, every few years, to finding that machines have yet another skill we once took for granted to be uniquely human. We can look forward to continued waves of disruption in how we live our lives, work for a living, educate ourselves and connect to our fellow humans. Job displacement will accelerate, but the creation of new jobs – requiring a different, frequently more advanced skills than you may have today – will accelerate as well, as greater productivity generates greater momentum in the economy.

What is a community to do? What is the single most important job for the leaders of a community to take upon themselves, if they want the place called home to thrive?

They need to lean into the light.

The globalization of markets, the impact of the Near-Zero economy on business and individuals and the urgent need to become ever more productive – these profound forces have two starkly different sides. They are granting us big gains in wealth, health, learning and all manner of other good things – but mostly for those who standing in the light, the ones who know how to seize their benefits. For those who do not, they throw an ominous shadow over the future.

No community controls its own destiny. It is part of a state or province, part of a nation. It has its own history to contend with and stands united or divided based on events and decisions long past. But starting today, its leaders can lean into the light and help their people to do the same.

They can start doing what works in the 21st Century and stop doing what does not. They can bring about disciplined, energetic collaboration among business, government and institutions that breaks through the traditional barriers separating them. They can help their people understand the realities of the global economy and engage them in creating a better future. And they can insist that every worker at every level of qualification becomes the most skilled, educated and motivated in the world. They can work without ceasing to attract and keep the growing businesses and nonprofits that need those workers' labor.

Not every community will house a university, just as not every child needs to attend one. Even Google, that archetype of the new economy, is willing to hire people with no college degrees, so long as they have what the company values much more: "general cognitive ability — the ability to learn things and solve problems," in the words of Laszlo Brock, who is in charge of hiring 100 new people for the company every week.[211] But every community has assets – infrastructure, institutions, businesses, knowledge and personal commitment – and must be prepared to connect them all and to inspire them all to work toward shared goals.

What has powered the success of Intelligent Communities in the first decade of the 21st Century will continue to do so, even as technology advances and markets globalize. If there was ever a time when government, business and institutions could prosper apart, each in its own comfortable silo, that time is gone forever. Like or not, we are all in the same business together. Call it the business of getting into heaven: helping to *increase* the need for skill in the world and making sure our people meet the need.

Appendix

How Intelligent Communities Grow Their Economies, Societies & Cultures

You probably know what a Smart City is. But what is an Intelligent Community? Do we really need another word for the same old thing?

We don't – but then, it is *not* the same old thing. "Smart" is about applying technology to make cities work better, faster and cheaper. It is like automating a factory. Install the sensors, cameras, computers and network connections. Integrate them with software and artificial intelligence. Better data leads to better decisions, and automation lets you do more with less. It's a win for the city, its residents and taxpayers.

But it's not good enough

Large or small, however, cities are not just collections of infrastructure. They are stories, living and breathing, and have their roots in the first decisions of people to settle there. The visible parts of the city – and today, the invisible elements of the digital web being weaved within it – are the outward signs of an inward spirit.

Cities also have economies that are buffeted by the winds of global change, and they need to continually adjust their course to take advantage of them. Without economic and job growth, it doesn't matter how smart your city is.

For all these reasons, we don't think that being Smart is nearly good enough. We think the real journey of the place called home should be from Smart to Intelligent.

From Smart to Intelligent

Here's an example. Traffic studies show that 30% of the cars in congested central business districts are looking for parking. So, if we can reduce the time they spend in that search, we should also be reducing congestion and air pollution. A Smart City will specify its requirements, do an RFP, select vendors, install systems and start sending data to apps on phones that direct drivers to available parking. Smart, right?

Intelligent means something more. It means engaging local universities and technical schools, entrepreneurs and established businesses as partners in planning and carrying out this innovation project. What can be sourced in the municipality or the region? Where is there expertise that can help? It also means engaging the public in helping determine how and where the innovation should happen.

Solving problems that matter

Intelligent takes longer. It is more complicated, because it requires so many different players to work together. But it improves the odds that the solution will actually solve a problem that matters, and that the solution delivers benefits far beyond its scope. Benefits like building the capacity of local companies in the fast-growing technologies of the Internet of Things. Like giving birth to a new university or community college department that turns out graduates skilled in those technologies. Like making the innovation project something that citizens brag about (or worry about), increasing their commitment to their community.

The ICF Method

The ICF Method dates from our first studies of communities wrestling with the challenges looming on the horizon of the digital revolution. Over the past 20 years, it has been refined and improved by their experiences and has shaped the analytic tools we use to track them.

The Method is a way to *think differently* about the economic, social and cultural future of the place called home. It asks the leadership of communities to be both *visionary* – imagining previously impossible outcomes – and *practical*, adding new items to their long priority lists and ensuring that these things get done.

We do not usually talk about economic, social and economic growth in the same breath. Making money is making money: what can it have to do with the rest? But a moment's thought makes clear that a healthy economy is the necessary condition for a healthy society and an active culture that looks not just to the past but expresses optimism about the future. When the money runs out, it's hard for the people of a community to hang together. When they do, it is mostly in opposition to the outside world that has done them wrong, and the culture they share looks backward to better times, real or imagined, instead of forward. Economic, social and cultural health are the three pillars on which a good quality of life depends, one that makes the community a great place to live, work, start a business, raise a family and guide the next generation to maturity. Take away any one of them, and the foundation begins to crumble.

The core idea behind the Method is that there is a new way to conduct economic development in the digital age – a way that produces much greater success and also strengthens the social and cultural pillars of the community. It consists of six Factors that contribute to that virtuous cycle. Three of them drive growth in the economy, which powers every other thing of value in a community. Three of them are about caring for the community as it grows. They sustain its growth and manage the inevitable bad effects it brings, so as to preserve the quality of life that means so much to the people who live there and help attract and retain talented people and the organizations who employ them.

THE ICF METHOD

Six interrelated Factors that drive economic growth

© 2019 Intelligent Community Forum

High-speed connections for computers and mobile devices are the infrastructure no community can do without. Through those connections come employment opportunities, education, commerce, information, entertainment and community participation. Businesses depend on them to manage their operations, reach customers and attract employees. Governments rely on them to generate and analyze massive amounts of data to improve decision-making. Citizens use them to organize and coordinate, share ideas and build community spirit. Connected digital infrastructure including sensors and cameras that make possible machine learning and Internet of Things (IoT) applications that deliver better services for less money to more people and organizations.

WORK The well-paying work of the 21st Century is knowledge work. All opportunity for meaningful employment has shifted to those with skills, from the construction trades and automated factories to technology, finance and business management. Those without the right skills are increasingly being left behind. Intelligent Communities create a knowledge-based workforce through strong and continuing collaboration among local government, employers and schools. Together, they turn education into a ladder of opportunity teaching skills that are in demand and connecting young people with opportunities in the region to strengthen the community's economic and social foundation.

INNOVATE The economist Robert Solow won the Nobel Prize in 1987 for proving that 80% of all economic growth comes from developing and using new technology. That's a stunning number. It means that if the employers, institutions and government of your city or county are not creating new opportunities or putting new technology to work, you are missing out on 80% of the potential growth in today's economy. That's why every place needs an innovation strategy, which may range from tech clubs and hackathons to startup districts and IoT infrastructure.

ENGAGE To create change, you cannot afford to leave out the people of the community. They may not yet understand the challenges or have any idea how to tackle them. But they can become either the biggest obstacle to positive change or its most powerful advocates. Engaging people in the earliest stages of projects creates ownership. Ensuring that projects are designed and executed in a transparent and ethical manner builds trust. More than ever before, residents have digital tools at their disposal for developing coalitions, coordinating action and turning the fears or enthusiasms of a few people into a community-wide movement. That can drive your strategy forward or freeze it in its tracks.

INCLUDE The explosive advance of the digital economy has worsened the exclusion of people who already play a peripheral role in the economy and society, whether due to poverty, lack of education, prejudice, age, disability or location. It has also disrupted industries from manufacturing to retail services, enlarging the number of people for whom the digital revolution is a burden rather than a blessing. Effective digital inclusion targets access to technology and services, the issues of affordability and motivation to use digital technology and learn digital skills.

SUSTAIN Environmental sustainability is a global concern with local impact. It engages the community and generates action. When communities make sustainability a goal, they energize community groups, neighborhoods and community leaders with the promise of making a difference. Sustainability is also good for the economy. As the world is turning its attention to reining in human impact on the planet, sustainability is generating substantial new opportunities for technology advance, business growth and employment in green industries. It also helps communities achieve resilience in the face of environmental threats and human-caused emergencies.

* * * * *

These six Factors are *interdependent*: the success of each tends to support the success of the others. They are powerful in very large cities but even more so in small-to-midsize places, because change can come more easily when there are fewer key people and constituencies who must change their minds. They require *resources* but are also implemented one step at a time, so that each successful step helps produce more resources for the next.

Brain Gain

Index

Notes

[1] *Management: Tasks, Responsibilities, Practices* by Peter F. Drucker, Truman Talley Books / E.P. Dutton, 1986, page 128.

[2] "Worldwide, Good Jobs Linked to Higher Wellbeing" by Jon Clifton and Jenny Marlar, *Gallup World*, March 15, 2011 (http://www.gallup.com/poll/146639/worldwide-good-jobs-linked-higher-wellbeing.aspx)

[3] "Study Shows Psychological Impact of Unemployment" by Esme E. Deprez, *BusinessWeek*, September 3, 2009.

[4] "The Long Unemployed: Emotional Effects of Unemployment"by John M. Grohol, Psy.D., World of Psychology, PsychCentral.com (http://psychcentral.com/blog/archives/2011/09/19/the-long-unemployed-emotional-effects-of-unemployment)

[5] "Health hazards of unemployment–only a boom phenomenon?" by M. Novo, Λ Hammarstrom, U Janlert, Elsevier, 2000. (http://www.sciencedirect.com/science/article/pii/S0033350600003048)

[6] "Suicide Rates Up by 5,000 Because of 2008 Global Recession," by Christopher Harress, *International Business Times*, September 20, 2013.

[7] "The Psychological Consequences of Unemployment" by Deborah Belle and Heather E. Bullock," The Society for the Psychological Study of Social Issues Policy Statement (http://www.spssi.org/index.cfm?fuseaction=page.viewpage&pageid=1457)

[8] *The Contribution of Unemployment to Inequality and Poverty in OECD Countries*, by Rosa Martínez and Jesús Ruiz-Huerta (Universidad Complutense) and Luis Ayala (Universidad de Castilla-La Mancha), 2010. (www.alde.es/encuentros/anteriores/iiieea/autores/A/36.pdf)

[9] "Thousands Protest Auto Industry Job Losses," CBC News, May 27, 2007.

[10] Auto Job Losses Hurt Community" by Grace Macaluso, *The Windsor-Star*, December 19, 2008.

[11] "Labour Force Market Plan Report & Action Plan 2013-14," Workforce Windsor-Essex, April 9, 2013.

[12] "Spain's Youth Fleeing Country in Search of Work," by Ashifa Kassam, *The Toronto Star*, March 17, 2013.

[13] "Innovation and Economic Growth" by Nathan Rosenberg, Professor of Economics (Emeritus), Stanford University, Organization for Economic Co-operation and Development, 2004.

[14] *Management: Tasks, Responsibilities, Practices* by Peter F. Drucker, Harper & Row, 1973.

[15] "Does Innovation Stimulate Employment? A Firm-Level Analysis Using Comparable Micro-Data from Four European Countries" by Rubert Harrison, Jordi Jaumandreau, Jacques Mairesse and Bettina Peters, National Bureau of Economic Research Working Paper 14216, August 2008.

[16] "Jobless Recovery Leaves Middle Class Behind" by Chrystia Freeland, Reuters, *The New York Times*, April 12, 2012.

[17] "Jobless Recovery Leaves Middle Class Behind."

[18] "Automatic Reaction," *The Economist*, September 9, 2010.

[19] "An Existential Crisis for Law Schools" by Lincoln Caplan, The New York Times, July 14, 2012.

[20] "Automatic Reaction."

[21] "Automatic Reaction."

[22] "List of companies by revenues," Wikipedia, http://en.wikipedia.org/wiki/List_of_companies_by_revenue

[23] "Highest-Paid Actors 2012 – Hollywood's Top-Earners," The Richest.org, http://www.therichest.org/money/forbes-highest-earning-actors/

[24] "J.K. Rowling," Wikipedia http://en.wikipedia.org/wiki/J._K._Rowling.

[25] "America's Highest Paid CEOs" by Scott DeCarlo, *Forbes*, April 4, 2012.

[26] "The Future of Middle-Skill Jobs."

[27] *Menial is Menial No More*, Ontario Literacy Coalition, October 25, 2011

[28] *Menial is Menial No More.*

[29] *Skills Supply and Demand in Europe: Medium-Term Forecast Up to 2020*, European Centre for the Development of Vocational Training, Publications Office of the European Union, 2010.

[30] "Job Outlook, By Education, 2006-2016" by Drew Liming and Michael Wolf, *Occupational Outlook Quarterly*, Fall 2008.

[31] "1969 – Chattanooga Most Polluted City in the United States," Air Pollution Control Bureau Internet of Things site, March 28, 2014 (http://apcb.org/about/history.aspx)

[32] *2012/2013 Annual Report on European SMEs*, The European Commission, 2013.

[33] "Frequently Asked Questions," SBA Office of Advocacy (www.sba.gov/sites/default/files/FAQ_Sept_2012.pdf).

[34] "Credit Score, by Multiple Choice," by Sarah Wheaton, *The New York Times*, December 31, 2013

[35] *SMEs in Turbulent Times – A Comparative Analysis Between Argentina, Brazil and European Countries* by Carolin Häner, University of Applied Sciences, Wiesbaden Business School, October 15, 2011.

[36] *Job Creation in America: How Our Smallest Companies Put the Most People to Work,* by David Birch, 1987.

[37] *Key Statistics: Australian Small Business*, Department of Innovation, Industry, Science and Research, Government of Australia, 2011.

[38] *Key Small Business Statistics: August 2013*, Industry Canada SME Research and Statistics (http://www.ic.gc.ca/eic/site/061.nsf/eng/02802.html)

[39] "Hunting for Gazelles" by Joshua Zumbrun, *Forbes*, October 30, 2009.

[40] "The Engines of Growth" by Brian Blackstone and Vanessa Fuhrmans, *The Wall Street Journal*, June 27, 2011.

[41] Ibid.

[42] "Germany's Mittelstand: Beating China," *The Economist*, July 20, 2011.

[43] "Germany's Secrets for a Steadier Job Market," by Jack Ewing, *The New York Times*, April 21, 2010.

[44] "Who Needs Casinos? Five Ideas to Rev Up Communities," by Shane Dingman, *The Globe and Mail*, August 22, 2013.

[45] "A Snowier Silicon Valley in BlackBerry's Backyard," by Ian Austen, *The New York Times*, December 22, 2013.

[46] "Social Mobility," Wikipedia (https://en.wikipedia.org/wiki/Social_mobility).

[47] Khan Academy," Wikipedia (http://en.wikipedia.org/wiki/Khan_Academy).

[48] "KhanAcademy," Wikipedia.

[49] *World Broadband Statistics Q2 2012*, PointTopic, October 2012.

[50] *Traffic and Market Report on the Pulse of the Networked Society*, Ericsson, June 2012.

[51] "When People Worry about Math, the Brain Feels the Pain" by William Harms, *UChicago News*, October 31, 2012 (http://news.uchicago.edu/article/2012/10/31/when-people-worry-about-math-brain-feels-pain)

[52] "Massive Open Online Course," Wikipedia, (http://en.wikipedia.org/wiki/Massive_open_online_course).

[53] "ALISON," Wikipedia, (http://en.wikipedia.org/wiki/ALISON_%28company%29).

[54] "Massive Open Online Course," Wikipedia.

[55] "Not Staying the Course" by Chris Parr for *Times Higher Education*, Inside Higher Ed, May 10, 2013.

[56] "After Setbacks, Online Courses Are Rethought," by Tamar Lewin, *The New York Times*, December 10, 2013.

[57] Ibid.

[58] "The Rise of Megacities" by Nick Mead and the Guardian interactive team, *The Guardian*, October 4, 2012 (www.theguardian.com/global-development/interactive/2012/oct/04/rise-of-megacities-interactive).

[59] *The State of World Population: Unleashing the Potential of Urban Growth*, United Nations Population Fund, 2007.

[60] "The Density of Innovation" by Richard Florida, *The Atlantic*, September 2010.

[61] "How the Great Reset Has Already Changed America" by Richard Florida, *The Atlantic*, July 2011.

[62] *Urban World: Mapping the Economic Power of Cities* by Richard Dobbs, Sven Smit, Jaana Remes, James Manyika, Charles Roxburgh and Alejandra Restrepo, McKinsey Global Institute, March 2011.

[63] "Can Motown be Mended?," *The Economist*, July 27, 2013.

[64] "Manchester," Wikipedia, August 9, 2013 (http://en.wikipedia.org/wiki/Manchester).

[65] "Ruhr," Wikipedia, August 10, 2013 (http://en.wikipedia.org/wiki/Ruhr).

[66] "1997 Asian Financial Crisis," Wikipedia, August 10, 2013 (http://en.wikipedia.org/wiki/1997_Asian_financial_crisis).

[67] "Should Philadelphia's Suburbs Help Their Central City?" by Robert P. Inman, *Business Review*, Federal Reserve Bank of Philadelphia, Q2 2003.

[68] *The State of World Population: Unleashing the Potential of Urban Growth*, United Nations Population Fund, 2007.

[69] "Taiwan: the convenience store capital of the world," *Taiwan Insights*, September 24, 2010.

[70] "Direct China-Taiwan Flights Begin," *BBC News*, July 4, 2008.

[71] "Taiwan's airports benefit from growth in 'cross-straits' traffic," Anna.Aero, January 18, 2012

[72] "Gateway to the World" by Kelly Her, *Taiwan Review*, May 1, 2011.

[73] "Ghost Towns on the Increase as Rural America Accounts for Just 16% of Population," *The Daily Mail*, July 28, 2011.

[74] "India's Massive Migration Crisis," Interview with K. Laxmi Narayan, Allianz Open Knowledge, October 18, 2011.

[75] "China's Young Rural-to-Urban Mirants: In Scarch of Fortune, Happiness and Independence," by Xiaochu Hu, Migration Policy Institute, January 4, 2012.

[76] "Gloomy France," by Pascal Bruckner, *City Journal*, Winter 2014.

[77] Ibid.

[78] Ibid.

[79] "So Much Fun. So Irrelevant," by Thomas L. Friedman, *The New York Times*, January 3, 2012.

[80] "Canada Breaks 100,000-student Ceiling for First Time," ICEF Monitor, March 13, 2013.

[81] "Chinese Students Boost US Univerisites to All-Time High Foreign Enrollment," by Associated Press, PBS Newshour, November 11, 2013.

[82] "Biggest Brain Drains: India Gets Nearly Two-Thirds of US H-1Bs," by Marcus Chan, Bloomberg News, August 20, 2013.

[83] "List of Countries by GDP (PPP) per Capita," Wikipedia, April 27, 2014.

[84] "Scale of NBN Disaster Revealed," by Annabel Hepworth and Mitchell Bingemann, *The Australian*, December 19, 2013.

[85] "3 Myths That Block Progress for the Poor," the 2014 Gates Annual Letter.

[86] *The Great Escape: Health, Wealth and the Origins of Inequality*, by Angus Deaton, Princeton University Press, 2013.

[87] *The 20th Century Transformation of U.S. Agriculture and Farm Policy*, by Carolyn Dimitri, Anne Effland and Nielson Conklin, US Department of Agriculture Economic Research Service, Economic Information Bulletin Number 3, June 2005.

[88] *Demographic Trends in Rural and Small Town America*, by Kenneth Johnson, Volume 1, Number 1 of Reports on Rural America, The Carsey Institute of the University of New Hampshire, 2006.

[89] United Nations Department of Economic and Social Affairs (http://esa.un.org/unup).

[90] "Rural Population Stagnates: Deaths Outpace Births in Many Counties, While Jobs Slump Deters Newcomers" by Conor Dougherty, *Wall Street Journal*, February 22, 2012.

[91] Geohive (http://www.geohive.com/earth/pop_urban2.aspx) 2010.

[92] "China's Urbanization: It Has Only Just Begun" by Dan Steinbock, Newgeography, December 2, 2012.

[93] "China's Urban Population Exceeds Countryside for First Time," *Bloomberg News*, January 17, 2012

[94] "Living with Hogs in Rural Iowa," *Iowa Ag Review,* Iowa State University, 2003.

[95] Productivity Commission, 1998, *The Australian Black Coal Industry*, Inquiry Report, AusInfo, Canberra, page 39.

[96] "Rural Population Stagnates: Deaths Outpace Births in Many Counties, While Jobs Slump Deters Newcomers" by Conor Dougherty, *Wall Street Journal*, February 22, 2012.

[97] *Lessons in Learning: The Rural-Urban Gap in Education*, Canadian Council on Learning, March 1, 2006.

[98] "Factors of population decline in rural areas and answers given in EU member states' strategies" by Karcagi Kovats Andrea and Katona Kovacs Judit, *Studies in Agricultural Economics* 114, 2012.

[99] "With Help Online, French Farmers Now Playing the Field" by Maia de la Baume, *The New York Times*, August 30, 2011.

[100] "Tibenham: A Norfolk Village," www.tibenham.fsnet.co.uk/rural_decline.htm

[101] "The Unhealthy Meat Market," by Nicholas Kristof, *The New York Times*, March 13, 2014.

[102] National Chicken Council, March 13, 2014.

[103] *The State of World Population: Unleashing the Potential of Urban Growth*, UNFPA, 2007.

[104] "Cities, Information and Economic Growth" by Edward L. Glaeser, *Cityscape*, US Department of Housing and Urban Development, Vol. 1, No. 1, Chapter 2.

[105] "Global Metropolis: The Role of Cities and Metropolitan Areas in the Global Economy," Martin Prosperity Institute, March 2009.

[106] *Guide to City Development Strategies: Improving Urban Performance*, The Cities Alliance, 2006 (www.citiesalliance.org/node/737)

[107] "Duh! 7 of 2010's most obvious scientific discoveries," *The Week*, December 30, 2010. http://theweek.com/article/index/210383/duh-7-of-2010s-most-obvious-scientific-discoveries

[108] "Clock's Ticking as Mumbai Struggles to Dispose of Waste" by Viju B and Sharad Vyas, *The Times of India*, June 5, 2011.

[109] "The Cheapest Generation" by Derek Thompson and Jordan Weissmann.

[110] "With Help Online, French Farmers Now Playing the Field."

[111] "Helping Start-Ups with Local Support and National Networks" by Sarah Max, *The New York Times*, February 8, 2013.

[112] "Helping Start-Ups with Local Support and National Networks."

[113] "America R.I.P.: Death of the Middle Class, Offshoring of American Jobs" by Dr. Paul Craig Roberts, Global Research, October 17, 2012.

[114] "The Changing Nature of Manufacturing in OECD Economies," by Dirk Pilat, Agnes Cimper, Karsten Olsen and Colin Webb, Directorate for Science, Technology & Industry, Organization for Economic Cooperation and Development, October 27, 2006.

[115] "Textile Plants Humming, but Not a Lot of Workers" by Stephanie Clifford, *The New York Times*, September 30, 2013.

[116] "Factory Output Returns, but at Widely Different Rates" by Floyd Norris, *The New York Times*, October 19, 2013.

[117] "Heading South: US-Mexico Trade and Job Displacement After NAFTA" by Robert E. Scott, Economic Policy Institute. May 3, 2011.

[118] *Macroeconomics* by Glenn Hubbard and Anthony P. O'Brien. Prentice Hall, 2006, 233-234.

[119] "So Much for the Scare Stories," *The Economist*, June 6, 2008.

[120] "Offshoring Creates as Many US Jobs as It Kills, Study Says," by Suzy Khimm, *The Washington Post*, July 12, 2012.

[121] "Gross World Product," Wikipedia, October 6, 2012 (http://en.wikipedia.org/wiki/Gross_world_product)

[122] "Outsourcing Not the Culprit in Manufacturing Job Loss" by Wes Iversen, *Automation World*, December 9, 2003.

[123] "Automation, Not Offshoring, Real Source of Manufacturing Job Loss" by SCDigest Editiorial Staff, *Supply Chain Digest*, June 12, 2008.

[124] "International Comparisons of Manufacturing Productivity and Unit Labor Cost Trends, 2011 Data Tables," US Bureau of Labor Statistics, December 6, 2012, Table 1.

[125] "Outsourcing Not the Culprit in Manufacturing Job Loss."

[126] *Made in America, Again: Why Manufacturing Will Return to the US*, by Harold L. Sirkin, Michael Zinser and Douglas Hohner, The Boston Consulting Group, August 2011.

[127] Ibid.

[128] "The Important Role Services Play in an Economy" by Cengiz Haksever and Barry Render, *The Financial Times*, July 25, 2013.

[129] "New Hackett Research Forecasts Offshoring of 750,000 More Jobs In Finance, IT, Other Key Business Services Areas by 2016," The Hacket Group, March 27, 2012.

[130] "Gross domestic product per capita by country and year, 1950-2015," Institute for Health Metrics and Evaluation (www.healthmetricsandevaluation.org) , 2013.

[131] Ibid.

[132] "After the Personal Computer," *The Economist*, July 6, 2013.

[133] Ibid.

[134], *America's Infrastructure Report Card 2009*, American Society of Civil Engineers.

[135] *2013 Report Card for America's Infrastructure*, the American Society of Civil Engineers.

[136] Economic Development Bureau, Taichung City Government (http://eng.taichung.gov.tw/mp.aspx?mp=6)

[137] "After the Personal Computer."

[138] "Charting Nokia's Decline," by Emily Cadman, *The Financial Times*, September 3, 2013.

[139] "Observations Concerning the Increase of Mankind, Peopling of Countries, etc." by Benjamin Franklin, 1751.

[140] "What Impact Did the Germany Immigrants Have on the US Economy in the 1800s?," Fox News, 2008.

[141] "Can Immigration Speed the Economy Recovery?" by Alain Sherter, *MoneyWatch*, September 12, 2013.

[142] "What Drives Success?" by Amy Chua and Jed Rubenfeld, *The New York Times*, January 25, 2014.

[143] "Rethinking the Effects of Immigration on Wages" by G. Ottavioano and G. Peri, NBER Working Paper 12497, 2006.

[144] "Immigration's Economic Impact," The White House Council of Economic Advisors, June 20, 2007.

[145] Ibid.

[146] "Immigrant Entrepreneurs and Small Business Owners, and their Access to Financial Capital," Robert W. Fairlie, Small Business Association Office of Advocacy, 2012.

[147] "Immigration's Economic Impact."

[148] "What Drives Success?" by Amy Chua and Jed Rubenfeld, *The New York Times*, January 25, 2014.

[149] "Foreign Entrepreneurs 'Disproportionately Contribute' to UK Economy, Says Luke Johnson," by Asa Bennett, *The Huffington Post UK*, November 18, 2013.

[150] *The Impact of Recent Immigration on the London Economy*, London School of Economists and Political Science, July 2007.

[151] "Immigrants: Better Than Billed," *The Economist*, December 22, 2012.

[152] "Immigration and the Public Finances: Boon or Burden?" *The Economist*, June 15, 2013.

[153] "List of Countries by Foreign-Born Population, Wikipedia, December 29, 2013 (http://en.wikipedia.org/wiki/List_of_countries_by_foreign-born_population)

[154] "Is Immigration Bad for the Economy? Many People Say Yes," by Matthew Scott, *Daily Finance*, September 12, 2010.

[155] "Don't Shut the Golden Door," by John H. MacDonald and Robert J. Sampson, *The New York Times*, June 19, 2012.

[156] *The Impact of Recent Immigration on the London Economy*.

[157] "New York City's Office for Immigrants Has Become a Global Model," by Kirk Semple, *The New York Times*, December 30, 2013.

[158] Ibid.

[159] "Immigrants Playing a Larger Role in City's Economy," by Daniel Massey, *Crain's New York Business*, January 13, 2010.

[160] "Central Ohio Benefits from Immigrants," The Columbus Dispatch, July 18, 2013.

[161] "Government Lacks Vision, System is Out-of-Date: Mayor," *Expatica*, DutchNews.nl, January 8, 2014.

[162] "Canada Immigration: How a Decade of Policy Change Has Transformed the Immigration Landscape," by Nicholas Keung, *The Toronto Star*, February 15, 2013.

[163] *The Influence of Immigrants on Trade Diversification in Saskatchewan*, The Conference Board of Canada, April 2013.

[164] "Immigrants Help Boost Canada's Innovation," By Nicholas Keung, *The Toronto Star*, October 14, 2010.

[165] "Why the World's Best and Brightest Struggle to Find Jobs in Canada," by Tamsin McMahon, *Maclean's*, April 24, 2013.

[166] *Understanding "Canadian Exceptionalism" in Immigration and Pluralism Policy*, by Irene Bloemraad, Migration Policy Institute of the Translatic Council on Migration, July 2012.

[167] "Canadians view immigration more positively than Europe, U.S.: poll," by Ian Shelton, *iPolitics*, February 3, 2011.

[168] "Why the World's Best and Brightest Struggle to Find Jobs in Canada."

[169] Local Immigration Partnership Toronto South, www.torontolip.com, January 2014.

[170] "Amsterdam has a Deal for Alcoholics: Work Paid in Beer," by Andrew Higgins, *The New York Times*, December 4, 2013.

[171] Science Museum UK, February 8, 2014. (www.sciencemuseum.org.uk/whoami/findoutmore/yourbody/whatdoyourcellsdo/howoftenareyourcellsreplaced.aspx)

[172] *Measuring the Information Society 2012*, International Telecommunications Union.

[173] "Police Win Praise in Riverside," by Tina Daunt, *Los Angeles Times*, December 26, 2002.

[174] "Muni Wi-Fi: Another One Bits the Dust?" by Colin Wood, *Governing,* February 4, 2014.

[175] "Birmingham City Council's Business Transformation Programme," West Midlands Regional Improvement and Efficiency Partnership, www.westmidlandsiep.gov.uk, March 2, 2014.

[176] Ibid.

[177] "St. Basil's Helps Develop Virtual Rucksack for Homeless," *Birmingham Post*, April 7, 2008.

[178] Digital Birmingham, www.digitalbirmingham.co.uk, March 2, 2014.

[179] "Birmingham City Council's Business Transformation Programme."

[180] "Crop Values Drop 9.8% in 2013 as Prices Fall," by David Pitt, Associated Press, *USA Today*, February 17, 2014.

[181] SDN Communications Internet of Things site, March 9, 2014, www.sdncommunications.com.

[182] South Dakota Network, LLC, Project Connect South Dakota , Broadband USA, www2.ntia.doc.gov/grantees/SDakotaNetwork

[183] "The Conversation: Responses and Reverberations," letter to the editor by John Goodman, *The Atlantic*, January/February 2014.

[184] "Creative Destruction: Newspaper Ad Revenue Has Gone into a Precipitous Free Fall, and It's Probably Not Over Yet," by Mark J. Perry, AEI Ideas, American Enterprise Institute, August 6, 2013.

[185] "The Humble Hero," *The Economist*, May 18, 2013.

[186] "Nextshoring: A CEO's Guide," by Kaley George, Sree Ramaswamy and Lou Rassey, *McKinsey Quarterly*, January 2014.

[187] "Printing a Bit of Me," *The Economist*, March 8, 2014.

[188188] "The Rise of Anti-Capitalism," by Jeremy Rifkin, *The New York Times*, March 15, 2014.

[189] "When the Wind Blows," *The Economist*, September 7, 2013.

[190] "The Rise of Anti-Capitalism."

[191] "Pixel and Dimed: On (Not) Getting By in the Gig Economy," by Sarah Kessler, *Fast Company*, March 18, 2014.

[192] "The Gig Economy is Here, and It's Not a Pretty Picture" by Stowe Boyd, GigaOm.com, March 31, 2014.

[193] "Google's Self-Driving Cars Complete 300k Miles Without Incident, Deemed Ready for Commuting," by Frederic Lardinosis, *TechCrunch*, August 7, 2012.

[194] "Google's Driverless Cars are Safer Than Vehicles Driven by Humans, But They Aren't Perfect," by Dana Dovey, *Medical Daily*, April 18, 2014.

[195] US Bureau of Labor Statistics.

[196] "Ghost Ships," *The Economist Technology Quarterly*, March 8, 2014.

[197] "Nextshoring: A CEO's Guide."

[198] Ibid.

[199] "Human-Machine Relations Changing, Says Gartner," by Mark Sutton, CommsEMEA, August 22, 2013.

[200] Ibid.

[201] Ibid.

[202] "The First News Report on the LA Earthquake Was Written by a Robot," by Will Oremus, Slate.com, March 17, 2014.

[203] "Professor: 90% of News Stories to be Written by Computers by 2030," Paul Joseph Watson, Infowars.com, March 24, 2014.

[204] "Labour Pains," *The Economist*, November 2, 2013.

[205] "Labor Force and Employment: 1800-1960," by Stanley Lebergott, Wesleyan University, *American Economic Growth and Standards of Living Before the Civil War*, University of Chicago Press, January 1992.

[206] *Steam Power, Establishment Size and Labor Productivity Growth in Nineteenth Century American Manufacturing* by Jeremy Atack, Fred Bateman and Robert Margo, National Bureau of Economic Research, January 2006.

[207] *Are Robots Taking Our Jobs, or Making Them?* by Ben Miller and Robert D. Atkinson, The Information Technology and Innovation Foundation, September 2013.

[208] "Economic Watch: The Top 10 Industries by Employment Growth," by Marcial Nava and Boyd Stacey, BBVA Research, September 27, 2013.

[209] "Taking on Adam Smith (and Karl Marx)," by Steven Erlanger, *The New York Times*, April 19, 2014.

[210] *Are Robots Taking Our Jobs, or Making Them?*

[211] "How to Get a Job at Google, Part 2," by Thomas L. Friedman, *The New York Times*, April 19, 2014.